PRAYERS FOR HEALING

MICHAEL HARPER is the Director of
Burrswood Christian Centre for Healthcare
and Ministry. Founded by Dorothy Kerin and
set in the beauty and tranquility of the Kent
countryside, it is a leading centre for the
Christian healing ministry in Britain.

MICHAEL FULLJAMES, an Anglican priest,
recently retired as the Chaplain of
Burrswood. He now lives in Canterbury.

PRAYERS
FOR HEALING

A Burrswood Companion

MICHAEL HARPER
and
MICHAEL FULLJAMES

CANTERBURY
PRESS
Norwich

©Michael Fulljames and Michael Harper 2003

First published in 2003 by
the Canterbury Press Norwich
(a publishing imprint of
Hymns Ancient & Modern Limited,
a registered charity)
St Mary's Works, St Mary's Plain,
Norwich, Norfolk NR3 3BH

www.scm-canterburypress.co.uk

British Library Cataloguing in Publication data

A catalogue record for this book is available
from the British Library

ISBN 1-85311-503-7

Typeset by Vera Brice
Printed and bound by
Biddles Ltd, www.biddles.co.uk

CONTENTS

FOREWORD

It is a privilege to commend this book of reflections and prayers, which is the fruit of a very close partnership between a priest and a doctor at Burrswood, where medical care and Christ's healing ministry are offered hand in hand.

Between them, the two Michaels have many years experience in general practice and parochial ministry, in hospices and hospitals (both general and psychiatric), and in the military and missions. They have learned not only to be professional, but also to be sensitive both to the suffering and the faithfulness of the people they have encountered and cared for along the way.

For most of us illness is part of our pilgrim journey on which God accompanies us whether we can feel his presence or not. In difficult and testing moments, holding on, when his guidance or healing is not easily discerned, demands courage and faith, endurance and hope.

What I have discovered in this book time and again is an encouragement not to duck, but to face painful realities and wrestle with issues, feelings, questions and doubts. Doing this in heart, thought and prayer leads to a renewed focus on God's healing purpose, discovering again the assurance of his presence and infinite compassion. This brings renewed trust, hope and peace.

I gladly commend *Prayers for Healing* to you, whether for yourself, or as you pray for those for whom you care.

+ JOHN PERRY
Bishop of Chelmsford

INTRODUCTION

The pain and surprise of disease deeply affects us. It affects our capacity to think and to pray. Our relationship with God is affected, sometimes for better, sometimes apparently for worse. We feel new emotions. Disease is truly all encompassing. It is not always easy to know which part of our being is most affected.

Our aim in this book is to provide morning reflections and evening prayers for each day of a month. We cover a range of topics, times and experiences commonly encountered. As we find no clear boundaries between thought and meditation, prayer and argument, there is inevitably some overlap between morning and evening.

All our individual experiences are different. What feels important to one means little to another. But we hope that you will recognise the common language of suffering, borne and wrestled with in these pages. Between us, in our humanity, we have gone through much of what we write, but not all. That which is outside our personal experience we have been enormously privileged to see at first hand as we have sat with those in need, especially those who have come to Burrswood to find God's healing.

We have tried to reflect with the mind, and feel from the heart. Some of this book is analytical, some is emotional, some yearning, some raw. In writing it together we have learned much from one another. Now we hope that you will add to it your own experience, your own prayers. May it not be a record of our thoughts and prayers; may it rather come alive as it serves as a catalyst for yours. And may Jesus be glorified in everything.

PRAYERS
FOR HEALING

MADE BY GOD

I will give thanks unto thee for I am fearfully and wonderfully made: marvellous are thy works, and that my soul knoweth right well.

Psalm 139.13 BCP

Lord, You have made us for Yourself, and our hearts are restless till they find their rest in You.
St Augustine

The more we learn about the way we are made, the more remarkable we discover ourselves to be. Most of us is out of sight; the amazing miracle of the working of genes and chromosomes and cells is well beyond our human imagination. To understand how subtle are the effects of heart and soul, mind and spirit, feelings, fears and desires is a challenge to all.

I was created to see God, and I have not yet accomplished that for which I was made.
St Anselm

When we think of ourselves as made by God, everything about our creation is even more wonderful. As the Psalmist makes clear in Psalm 139, to be known by God is truly awesome. It is not the partial knowledge and understanding of even the most discerning human parent. God is there, sees, knows, understands

A person made in God's image has a purpose – to be in relationship with God, who is there.
Francis Schaeffer

everything; he traces our footsteps, is aware of all our thoughts and actions. It could become a bit much! Sometimes we feel we'd like to get away from him for a while.

But the Psalmist knows that would give no peace. Accepting willingly that he is always there, and cares for us better than we can ourselves, let us choose to be thankful. Count it a blessing to go with him, letting him lay his hand upon us, to lead us, and keep close guard upon us.

My Lord, I thank you for having created me.
St Clare of Assisi

What a comfort and encouragement it is to know that we belong within his love; from before our conception God has known every detail of our being, and treasures us. His desire is to be in harmony with us, to make us the people he meant us to be from the very beginning. Then we shall know ourselves made whole.

MADE BY GOD

O Lord – *You know me completely –*
I am an open book before you!
You surround me on every side
in your loving kindness;
you know how I think
and what I am about to say.
Selah!

O Lord – *Wherever I go, you are there:*
I cannot escape you.
I cannot escape into darkness, even:
it is as day to you.
You see me.

My Lord! *All of me – warts and all!*
You see all; and yet you lead
and hold me wherever I go.
How? I am a sinner:
but you know that too.
You hold me in my times of shame.

O Lord – You have made me!
>   Every cell, every system
>   made in the secret place;
>   and you knew every day of my life
>   before it was.
>   My independence is an illusion!
>   I can choose to embrace you in
>   my heart, which you know so well,
>   or say to you – depart from me!
>   For I am a sinful person.
>   But you know that,
>   and love me still.
>   I quiver and melt. I melt. I melt.

O Lord – I want to know you more,
>   to know your thoughts,
>   to lay my head on your bosom
>   in rest and peace.
>   Teach me. Search me. Try me.
>   Lead me away from wrong paths
>   and into your way,
>   the way everlasting.
>   So I may be with you
>   for ever and ever.

Amen

CHRIST THE HEALER

After sunset all who had friends who were sick with various diseases brought them to Jesus; he placed his hands on every one of them and healed them all.

Luke 4.40 GNB

God so loved the world that He gave His only begotten son. Jesus so loved that He healed. Healings gave authenticity to His mission and His person.
Morton Kelsey

This testimony arises out of a meditation on Luke 5.17–26.

You would find it hard to imagine how I felt: totally paralysed, so helpless and dependent; I had to have everything – yes, everything – done for me. No wonder I agreed when they suggested taking me to the 'Healer'. Being carried along on the flat wasn't too bad, but up that outside staircase was pretty desperate. Then to be let down though the roof – even my friends looked uncomfortable – to find all those eyes on me.

But his eyes were so different, so full of love; such a depth of acceptance. He had looked up at my friends, seen something in their faces, had picked up their plea without a word being spoken; and then gave me his complete attention. His look said it all: total warmth, concern, compassion, understanding. It was if he knew me through and through, even the shame and guilt I'd been trying to deny; and still he accepted me – just as I was.

The healing of his seamless dress Is by our beds of pain; We touch him in Life's throng and press, And we are whole again.
J. G. Whittier

'My son,' he said, speaking personally, intimately, giving me the feeling he really cared; 'your sins are forgiven.' What: all of them, even . . . ? Yes, yes, yes! I felt the power and authority in his words. It was fantastic. It was as though shackles that had been binding me tight were suddenly broken, as though a great weight was lifted off my soul – and my body too. With my ears I was aware they were arguing theology, but I felt free. I was becoming aware of sensations in toes and fingers like I hadn't had for a very long while; something very wonderful indeed was happening to me.

Then he spoke to me again. He had been asking if they thought it was easier to forgive people's sins or to get a paralysed man to walk. I think he wanted to prove he had the right to forgive. To me he said, 'I tell you, get up, pick up your mat, and go home!' At that moment I would have done anything he asked, without any doubt. I knew I could. So I did: just like that. Was I happy? And was I a changed man? You bet; and I'd love you to know Jesus this way as well.

CHRIST THE HEALER

*'Lord Jesus Christ: you are the light
of the world:
your light and power and mercy leapt
to this man,
and by your grace he was forgiven
and healed.'*

I feel paralysed, too.
Life has come to a full stop.
And yet, my Lord, this man, he had been
lying on his stretcher for years.
All hope gone, all prospects of the joys of
life I can so easily take for granted.

'Dear Lord, when my faith burns low, hear the prayers of my friends and family; encourage them, and bless them as you touch me . . . '

He had no faith; his light had been
snuffed out. But you, Lord, saw the faith
of his friends.

You forgave his sins – 'My child, your
sins are forgiven.'

*'Dear Lord, I freely confess my sins.
I too think and speak amiss too often;
I do what I ought not to do and do not do
what I ought.
Forgive me, too; you know my heart.
I reach to you. In your mercy, reach down to
me,
forgive me, free me . . . '*

He rose and departed, glorifying God.

'Let there be glory
now, Lord! –
as I see your
glory, so will I
glorify you in
truth: let me see
your glory . . . '

And they were all amazed; they glorified
God and were filled with fear.

'Will you not let your power come?
For there is no glory to them in my
infirmity:
show your glory: show your glory, O Lord!
I may see your glory in your presence alone:
They would see it with their eyes, and
glorify you,
And believe . . . '

'And yet, Lord, in truth I know that if I
have you, I have all:
I would rather be a doorkeeper in your
house than spend my whole life somewhere
else. Let me put my hand in yours;
let me lay my head upon your breast and
find my rest.
But best of all, may I be healed in all my
being.
Dear Lord, hear my prayer
and let my cry come to you.'

SUDDEN ILLNESS

'Remember your Creator . . . before the silver
cord is loosed, or the golden bowl is broken,
or the pitcher shattered at the fountain, or
the wheel broken at the well . . . '

Ecclesiastes 12.6 RAV

*The future has a
habit of suddenly
and dramatically
becoming the
present.*
Roger Ward
Debson

*Time has tapped
me on the
shoulder.*
Anatole Broyard

Sudden illness is rude. It is forced upon one, literally, and demands absolute attention. Often it appears out of a clear blue sky – it interrupts life in full flow. It laughs at negotiation: it just is. We have it, like it or not. It threatens us, weakens us and frightens us. It is a megaphone to silence the whispers of complacency. Mortality arrives by express and knocks at our door.

I've been licked by the flames; my sense of self has been singed.
Anatole Broyard

Sudden illness casts a shadow over us. It brooks no delay; it ushers in white coats, needles, drips, questions, examinations and anxious faces. Huddled conversations with family members blossom into expansive medical smiles – Hello! How are you feeling now? We'll get you right soon. 'Dear God, be here. He's too attentive for my liking. Dear God, be here: I hurt. That's a big needle: what is she going to do with it? Dear God, be here. Am I survivor or a casualty? Or in a dream? Surround me, Lord' – and he does. He does.

I had dawdled through life up to that point . . . all my old trivial selves fell away, and I was reduced to essence. I began to look around me with new eyes . . .
Anatole Broyard

Sudden illness changes us. No longer can we pretend immortality with integrity. It is like surviving a plane crash: life is thereafter different. We traverse its night with the flashlight of anxiety, and, when we espy the dawn, we breathe a sigh of relief. Yet we know – the night will return, and the day may be shorter. Then, if I cannot presume upon life everlasting in this flesh, what must I do first? Where are my priorities?

SUDDEN ILLNESS

*Remember your Creator . . . before the days
of trouble come. Remember him before the
pitcher is shattered at the fountain . . . and
the spirit returns to God who gave it.*

From Ecclesiastes 12

I have survived and arrived in that place
where everyone smiles, and says,
How well you look! And I've
brought some flowers (no chocs!).
And they punch my chin and say
In no time you'll be fine.

But I've received a blow, Lord,
and how it knocked me off
my feet! Yet I'm feeling
my way to praying, Lord.
Hold me tight, and let your light
illuminate my way.

It isn't easy to discover
weakness, Lord. I thank
you for your love, and I remember you
before the silver cord is
loosed: grant me strength
to love, grant me patience
in weakness, and show me
your face.
I want to shine for you
whilst the day lasts: it
will pass; the pitcher will
shatter at the fountain.
In time.
But I have breath, and I have life;
let me shine for you.

THE CONSULTATION

The Lord has created medicines from
the earth,
and a sensible man will not
disparage them.
Was it not a tree that sweetened water
and revealed the power of the Lord?
The Lord has imparted knowledge to men
that by their use of this marvel he may
win praise.

Ecclesiasticus 38.4–6a NEB

The doctor: greatest ally? Or greatest fear? I am abandoned to this one to whom I have been referred, and about whom I know almost nothing. What would I want to know? A rank on a performance table? That would be comforting. But perhaps most of all, I want a *meeting.* I want to be taken into his, or her, heart. I want to be understood; not to be a 'case', for I do not see myself as that. May this doctor see me for who I am – as a whole person, body, mind and spirit.

*There may come a time when your recovery
is in their hands; then they too will pray to
the Lord to give them success . . .*
Ecclesiasticus 38.13–14a NEB

Yet the Lord is sovereign and rules in the
affairs of mankind: he knows my fears,
and will prepare the path. Hear my
prayer, O Lord! If I must fall into human
hands, let them be directed by my King:
let my doctor's mind harmonise with
my Creator's; may he or she be a blessing and be blessed. As for me, I put my
trust in you, King of the Universe . . .

THE CONSULTATION

*Now, Lord, you have kept your promise,
and you may let your servant go in peace.
With my own eyes I have seen your
salvation, which you have prepared in the
presence of all peoples:
A light to reveal your will to the Gentiles
and bring glory to your people Israel.*

Nunc Dimittis, Luke 2.29–32 GNB

How often, dear Lord, have those words
been part of my evening prayers – been
part of our Evensong worship, just before
we declare our faith in you, and go on to
make our intercessions, trusting you. This
is a precious part of our faith inheritance.

Ever-caring Lord, I thank you for the
comfort faithful Simeon's prayer has
given to millions of your faithful people,
in so many circumstances, through the
ages. When we have made his words our
words we have known the assurance that
you provide glimpses of salvation and
healing, blessing us with peace and light,
whether it has been a good day or bad,
joyful or sad, fearful or hopeful.

Today, Lord, seemed to have all those elements in it. Waiting for an appointment

can be very dreary – those awesome corridors – sitting there wondering why so many people spend so much time walking backwards and forwards. Thank you that I could pray while I waited. I'm sure it helped me to feel more sympathetic to the specialist.

You are my defender and my protector. You are my God; in you I trust. Keep me, and those for whom I pray, safe from all hidden dangers and from all deadly diseases. Cover us with your wings, that we may be safe, safe in your care and your faithfulness. Yes; and Amen.
Psalm 91.2–4, paraphrased

Nevertheless, merciful Lord, I have to confess I so easily get tongue-tied, and I seem to freeze when the news is not good, and while the topic was technical stuff my mind seemed to whirl. I thank you that I wasn't on my own, and I praise your holy name that you, too, were really present all the time, understood what I didn't, and by your Holy Spirit can remind us of things that are hard to recall.

Comforting Lord, I thank you that the doctors do listen to my reactions and my questions, do try with care to explain, desire to do the best for me and genuinely want a good outcome. Gracious Lord, in all that is being done, help me to trust them as the agents of your healing power, whether or not they know your inspiration.

As I have put myself in their hands today, so, Lord, I commend myself to your greater protection this night.

DIAGNOSIS

*O Lord, you have searched me
and known me . . .
It was you who formed my inward parts;
you knit me together.*

Psalm 139.1,3 NRSV

*Uncertain ills
torment us most.*
Seneca (4BC–AD65)

Diagnosis of necessity entails our facing fears. We are submitted to the diagnostic process as soon as we see a doctor – indeed, before then. Our neighbours and friends look at us and eye us up: they knew someone like us. Worryingly, these apocryphal figures so often are 'dead within a year . . . ' Better perhaps to have a proper diagnosis! So we set out on a trip to the doctor, who pushes, pokes and prods with question and fingers, who looks critically; and so often concludes with an idea, but only that. Diagnosis might depend upon a test or a tissue biopsy ('he wants a bit of me to look at under a microscope'). So I need blood taken, and a referral to a specialist, and perhaps an X-ray and that biopsy. And a large injection of faith. It all takes too long.

Yet the Lord knows. He knows. He made me, he knows how I function – and how I malfunction. I have the deepest longing

We are all
impatient of
uncertainty,
either in opinion
or conduct.
A. Maclaren

for a miracle, to be able to say, 'I was bright yellow and now I am healthy pink. Look what the Lord has done!' I am impatient and afraid.

Diagnosis is the fulcrum for our fears. It is not just the present; it is the future that we fear. It is not just limitations; it is treatment. It is not just the uncertainty of the diagnostic process; it is the discomfort and indignity. How may we face them?

*In your book were
written all the
days that were
formed for me,
when none of
them as yet
existed.*
Psalm 139.16
NRSV

We can only reflect that God, who has brought us thus far, will be our companion on the road.
We can only wait on him in humility, seeking the Lord and his way for us.
We can only let him into our situation, calling upon him for mercy, courage and strength in whatever measure they may be necessary.

Yet we can also pray that most powerful of prayers:

*It is the Lord who
goes before you;
he will be with
you, he will not fail
you nor forsake
you; do not fear
or be dismayed.*
Deuteronomy 31.8
NRSV

'Lord, let me fulfil all your purposes for me in this body. Let nothing fall to the ground undone.'

It can only be in his great eternal sustaining, through uncertainty and even, in due time, death itself, that we find peace. So we struggle to nestle in him, and pray that the struggling will decrease and the nestling will increase.

5 DIAGNOSIS

Just as I am, poor, wretched, blind;
Sight, riches, healing of the mind,
Yea, all I need, in thee to find,
O Lamb of God, I come.

Charlotte Elliott

As tenderly as a good father treats his children, so you, Lord, treat those who reverence you; you know of what we are made, you remember that we are dust.
After Psalm
103.13, 14

Lord God, I feel like an open book – visible to the inquisitive eye – known to others better that I am known to myself. With their clever machines and scans they look right through me – literally – but do they see the real me in those ghostly images?
With bio-chemistry they can tell me so much about my bodily functions; though not about the state of my soul.

Lord, I praise you for their discernment and their knowledge.
Lord, I thank you when the diagnosis is better than it might have been;
Lord, I look to you for comfort and company when it is worse than I feared. And yet, Lord, the not knowing was worse.
When it is still not clear, lead me, Lord, through the mists of uncertainty.
Whatever the implications, grant me, I pray, the strength to remain faithful;
in all things assisting me to nestle within your divine purposes, again and again.

Lord, let me fulfil all your purposes for me in this body. Let nothing fall to the ground undone.

Lord God, you look through me, too, as you always have. You see everything, know and understand me through and through in awesome clarity: all the fears and fantasies, motives and mistaken notions. You know of what I'm made, what I've done with it and how I've cared for myself. When I realise what your diagnosis is, I realise my need of medicine for the soul. Lord, have mercy, Christ, have mercy, Lord, have mercy.

It is the God who said, 'Let light shine out of darkness', who has shone in our hearts to give us the light of the knowledge of the glory of God in the face of Christ. But we have this treasure in earthen vessels, to show the transcendent power belongs to God and not to us.
2 Corinthians 4.6, 7

Lord God, I thank you that you have given me the insight into my needs.
I thank you for the self-knowledge you give.
I pray you, let me know my limitations in this testing, not just in body, but in heart and spirit too.

As I reflect, Lord God, on all you now reveal to me about myself, I realise I must praise you that most of me, body and soul, has worked as you meant it to from the very beginning when you formed me. In the total context of my life there have been relatively few bodily ills to hinder your godly works.

Lord God, I praise you that in most of my living and being I have had the chance to respond to your love and your calling, to grow in holiness as well as in healthiness, in grace as well as in wholeness.

I acclaim your presence, your reality in my life, Christ in me, the hope of glory. Now may I know as I am known. Alleluia!

PAIN

*After flogging Jesus, he handed him over
to be crucified.*

Matthew 27.26

*'I am poured out like water . . . all my
bones are out of joint . . . my heart has
turned to wax . . . my strength is dried up
like the potsherd . . . my tongue sticks to the
roof of my mouth; you lay me in the dust of
death. A band of evil men have encircled
me, they have pierced my hands and feet. I
can count all my bones . . . '*

Psalm 22.14–16 NIV

*When pain is to
be borne, a little
courage helps
more than much
knowledge, a little
human sympathy
more than much
courage, and the
least tincture of
the love of God
more than all.*
C. S. Lewis

I am gripped by pain.

I can cope with the usual everyday pains;
but this – this is relentless. It's always
there.

I am afraid that it might get worse, and I
shall be overwhelmed, and I am afraid to
think what might be causing it. I am
afraid . . . Why must I suffer?

Yet I have seen the goodness of the Lord:
I have known it often. He is the potter; I
am the clay, and I know in my mind that
he knows best.

I know that in times when all has been
well I have not stayed close to the Lord;

at times I have wandered, and God has been distant. Now I cry out to him and know my need of his closeness and touch.

I cannot keep telling others.
They mean well but they cannot understand.
                    I need the Lord.
                        I need the Lord.
                            I need the Lord.

Felt weakness deepens dependence on Christ for strength each day. The weaker we feel, the harder we lean. And the harder we lean, the stronger we grow spiritually, even while our bodies waste away . . .
J. I. Packer

I prefer independence; but now I need the doctors, too. I need them to know the Lord working through them . . . and I want them to know that they are the Lord's servants for me . . . that they might be encouraged – I am sure they need it . . .

And I need the Lord to give me serenity . . . to help me when I feel irritated and snappy with the very people who weep for me . . . who pour out their lives for me . . . who are so concerned for me . . . they, as well as I, need to know that God is in charge. There! – I've said it! God is in charge; he has reminded me . . .

God is in charge (help me to believe it).
God is in charge (help me to know it).
God is in charge; thank you, Lord.

I want to be where he is . . . to be caught up with him, in him; to know him close.

He knows. I remember the cross. I had forgotten; how he knows!

PAIN

My Lord, be close . . .

This pain is ever with me; I cannot get away from it,
and I fear that the only way I can cope is if you are as near as the pain.

Forgive me, Lord; I know that you are closer to me than I can ever know; that your Holy Spirit resides within my very being. Yet I need to *know* you close; Lord, hear my prayer, and let my cry come to you.

For my part, I draw close to you. Forgive me for the times when I have wandered far away, forgive, forgive. I love you, my Lord.

Send to me, I pray, just one or two to whom I can pour out my heart; ones who will not feel they need to correct me, to explain theological points, to put me right; and help me to pour forth no bitterness, nothing to prove a hurdle to them.

Thank you, Lord, for doctors and nurses. I value them more than I used to! Bless them and be with them as they reflect your mercy and tenderness.

And grant me peace – deep, inward peace, that all my words be full of peace. How can you use me but through my words? Let them be yours, my Lord, and let them bless those who hear them.

I need you, Lord . . . I cry out to you, O Lord my God . . . answer me and deliver me in the way you choose . . . guard me from bitterness and keep me in your ways and close to your heart . . . and grant me the peace that passes understanding . . . in Jesus' name. Amen

GOING INTO HOSPITAL

*A large crowd of sick people were lying in the
porches – the blind, the lame, and the
paralysed. A man was there who had been ill
for thirty-eight years. Jesus saw him lying
there, and he knew the man had been ill for
such a long time; so he asked him,
'Do you want to get well?'*

John 5.3–6 GNB

*Jesus went to the
Garden of
Gethsemane to
wait upon the out-
come. Waiting can
be the most intense
and poignant of all
human experiences
– the experience
which, above all
others, strips us
of our needs, our
values, and
ourselves.*
John Vanstone

Waiting lists for hospital admissions
today are huge. The man at the Pool of
Bethesda would no doubt have said that
it is the time you wait which is more
important. But perhaps the way you are
respected as a person and the quality of
the treatment is even more important,
whether in a twenty-first-century hospital
cubicle or a first-century poolside cubicle. In any case the waiting is a testing
time.

The day comes when we go into hospital
– with a strange mixture of feelings.
It may be in so many circumstances:
• for the first time in over seventy years,
or the umpteenth in twenty years
• after a long wait; and worrying if that
precious bed will still be free
• for a happy event, new life to be born
into this world

• facing the possibility of not coming home again
• in confusion or feeling disturbed, even being sent to a 'place of safety'
• in sudden pain or trauma, and in shock.

It can be with great relief or with a turmoil of feelings and questions that we enter the hospital doors. What exactly will happen to me? How will my dearest cope? What about bearing pain, and the indignities we suffer? Will they listen to me?

Being mostly unused to being hospital patients, we want reassurance, not only about our sickness and its related suffering, but also about being able to keep our personal integrity intact. Despite uncertainties and fears we want to retain hopefulness. Despite some incapacity we want to retain our identity.

Usually we feel as though we go in alone, despite the human company with us in Outpatients or in the ward. Amongst all those who meet us, speak to us, attend us we can know there is one who greets us asking, 'Do you want to get well?' Through his own wounds borne upon the cross that one has the power to work through all the medications, surgery and treatments.

Jesus said to him, 'Get up, pick up your mat and walk.' Immediately the man got well; he picked up his mat and started walking.
John 5.8–9 GNB

GOING INTO HOSPITAL

*Lord God, this is the day new patients come
into this ward.
I know how they are feeling,
uncertain, strange, apprehensive,
nervous, worried, downright afraid.*

William Barclay

*You, Lord, are a
refuge for the
oppressed, a place
of safety in times
of trouble.
Those who know
you, Lord, will
trust you; you do
not abandon
anyone who
comes to you.*
Psalm 9.9–10 GNB

Today, Lord, I thank you that when I feel uncertain I may be sure of you; one to whom I may come for security, comfort and strength.

Today, Lord, when it all feels strange, even smells funny, and I'm not sure what to do or how to behave, grant me, I pray, the assurance of your presence and understanding.

Today, Lord, if I feel I'm turning into an interesting case, or a set of symptoms, or merely a diagnosis, allow me, I pray, to remember you hold me to you as your beloved.

Lord God, as I realise more and more all that is going on here I want to thank you and praise you for this hospital, and those employed here:

*From thee all skill
and science flow,
All pity, care and
love,
All calm and
courage, faith and
hope;
O pour them from
above.*
Charles Kingsley

for all those who are so busy, scurrying back and forth, wanting to do their best for people who are sick or in great need;

for all who with tenderness and care are looking after those who are very frail, or near the end of their mortal life;

for the many who do dirty or dreary jobs just to see we are warm and fed, and our records are in order, and everything else is done that this place needs;

for those whom you've blessed with great clinical skill or therapeutic insight, and all who enable our healing processes to work out well.

*Into your
hands, O Lord,
I commend
my spirit.
Keep me as the
apple of your eye:
hide me under
the shadow of
your wings.*
Psalm 17.8 CW

Lord God, for all of us, your children, who are patients this night in hospital, hospice or nursing home, I pray grant your blessing and your peace, grant restful sleep and refreshment, grant us answers to our prayers for those we love and care about; and give grace and alertness to those who watch over us and meet our needs this night. Lord God, all these my prayers I offer thankfully in the name of Jesus. Amen

TREATMENT

*The Lord created medicines out of the earth
and the sensible will not despise them.*

Ecclesiasticus 38.4 NRSV

*Every patient
needs mouth to
mouth resuscita-
tion, for talk is
the kiss of life.*
Anatole Broyard

Treatment is a balancing act between
beneficial effect and possible side effect.
Treatment is also about absolute trust.
My doctor, my consultant, considers that
I would benefit from this treatment, or
that treatment. How do I react? How
much do I take at face value? How much
do I question? How willing is he or she
to enter into a dialogue with me about
my treatment?

Considering the options for treatment
demands clarity of thinking above all
else, and the clearest communication, in
both directions.

If I felt so inclined, would my doctor give
me references so I could examine the evidence for myself? Is this treatment
intended to be curative? – or to alleviate?
If only to alleviate or produce a tempo-
rary remission, at what cost, and for how
long? Would my consultant accept the
treatment in my situation? – and why?

I just wish my doctor would brood on my situation for perhaps five minutes, that he would give me his whole mind just once, be bonded with me for a brief space, survey my soul as well as my flesh, to get at my illness, for each man is ill in his own way.
Anatole Broyard

Can he or she enter into my situation? God grant us doctors who are able and willing to do so!

And in all this process, where is the Lord? We long for healing, full and complete, from the Lord; when we talk about treatment, can we still see him and trust in his purposes for our lives? Indeed, how should we pray? Perhaps the most powerful, and the most submitted, prayer would be that the Lord would allow us to fulfil all that he has determined for us; that nothing would fall to the ground because of illness or death. Yet this prayer gives up the demand for long life, vibrant health and joy, and instead focuses on God's will. It is a paradox, for our well-being and joy is in living out God's will, and living in his will we find closeness to him. And so we walk with him, hand in hand and heart to heart.

Jesus shows us the way. 'Let all things pass from me; yet not my will, but yours, be done.'

So it is that we steer our way around the treatment question. We pray for wisdom and discernment; yet at the end of the day the Lord knows his purposes for us. May they all be fulfilled, and may we not lose our joy and peace in believing.

TREATMENT

Jesus took the blind man by the hand and led him out of the village. After spitting on the man's eyes, Jesus placed his hands on him and asked him, 'Can you see anything?' The man looked up and said, 'Yes, I can see people, but they look like trees walking about.' Jesus again placed his hands on the man's eyes.This time the man looked intently, his eyesight returned, and he saw everything clearly.

Mark 8.23–25 GNB

*Praise the Lord, my soul, and do not forget how kind he is.
He forgives all my sins and heals all my diseases.*
Psalm 103.2–3
GNB

Praise to you, Lord Jesus: in your great mercy you have always known exactly the right treatment for our ills, both in body and soul.

Praise to you, Lord of heaven and earth: most of the treatments we have received through medical science and clinical care have worked pretty well.

There is no limit to the works of the Lord who spreads health over the whole world.
Ecclesiasticus 38.8
REB

Blessings upon you, Holy Spirit of compassion and love: for the knowledge and works of the surgeon and the dentist, the pharmacist and the physiotherapist; for the understanding and care in psychotherapy and the cure of souls; for the skills and solace of the physician and the nurse; for all whom you call to further your healing purposes. Inspire them, I pray, with your good counsel and wisdom.

Lord God, now that I face this treatment I confess my fears and my ignorance: I do not understand all the science behind it, and what it is really doing to me in the out of sight places; I am anxious about side effects and how it will affect me afterwards. I confess I worry that there is something I have not been told; or things they told me that I didn't pick up. Lord, have mercy.

Lord God, in all of this, pray be at my side; reassure my trembling heart and grant me to know your blessing on the means used, that with grace and confidence I may accept all that, in good conscience and for good reason, I have agreed to.

My urgent prayer to you, my Lord, is that I should be made well; that the treatments should work quickly to relieve pains and distress, to take away the disease.

My considered prayer to you, my Lord, is to ask that your will be done; whether I seem to be ill or well may your purposes be complete in me.

My Lord, I'm sure your will is for things to turn out well for me, as you encompass me in your salvation and wholeness. Lord of glory and grace, gratefully I commend myself, and those I love, into your hands and into your will, for now and for ever. Amen

PRAYER FOR MEDICAL STAFF

*Treat the doctor with the honour that is his
due, in consideration of his services;
for he too has been created by the Lord.*

Ecclesiasticus 38.1 NJB

*The best doctors
in the world are
Doctor Diet,
Doctor Quiet
and Doctor
Merryman.*
Jonathan Swift

Doctors used to be lifted high, on to pedestals. It is not a safe place to be, for pride comes before a fall. Relationships are now changing. Patients are only too well aware that medical staff, whether clinicians, nurses, para-medics, or other professionals allied to medicine, are fallible. Doctors are only too well aware that patients nevertheless have very high expectations.

In any relationship attitude and respect are crucial. A desire to take appropriate responsibility and a willingness to work together, sharing and facing realities, can ease the way to a good outcome in the widest sense. Good co-operation increases confidence; being able to trust those who treat us, whether we see much or little of them, helps us to be ready to benefit from their ministry. What can we do to assist this process? Sometimes

Then let the doctor take over – the Lord created him too – do not let him leave you, for you need him. There are times when good health depends on doctors.
Ecclesiasticus 38.
12–13 NJB

The Lord has brought forth medicinal herbs from the ground, and no one sensible will despise them. He uses these for healing and relieving pain; the druggist makes up a mixture from them.
Ecclesiasticus 38.
4–7 NJB

Healing itself comes from the Most High, like a gift received from a king.
Ecclesiasticus 38.2 NJB

there seems to be very little patient or carer can do: in severe emergency, waiting for results of tests, or during surgery. There are times when we are plainly just in their hands.

For the conscious believer prayer and intercession are always part of the process, not only for reassurance, but as the invocation of the divine healing grace. Although we may be unaware of the beliefs held by most of those who treat us, we can be sure that the Holy Spirit is not inhibited from assisting and inspiring people of sound learning, skill and integrity who wish to do what is right for their patients. As we are aware that so much depends now on teamwork we will pray, not only for individuals, but for good communications and harmonious relationships.

We can be ready to pray also for God's blessing on the means that are used, whether external therapies or drugs, herbal or chemical, which are all ultimately found or made using the resources of the created earth. If we say grace before our meals can we not also give thanks over the means of healing, even if humanly we may be reluctant to have to accept them? God has many means of helping his children.

PRAYER FOR MEDICAL STAFF

Blessed is the man whose strength is in you,
whose heart is set on pilgrimage.
As they pass through the valley of Baca,
they make it a spring;
the rain also covers it with pools.
They go from strength to strength;
every one of them appears before God
in Zion.

Psalm 84.5–7 RAV

Dear Lord, thank you for the team of caring people who look after me. Bless them for their care and sensitivity; be with them in the thinking they do – yet let them too have the release of knowing that, at the end of the day, you are in charge.

You are in charge! My spirit lifts!

Lord, how easily I succumb to the impression that they are in charge – that I am – anyone but you: and how depressed I then feel . . .

But it is you! – and at the very recognition of it something inside me takes to the air and is released, liberated . . .

For your eternal song serenades my soul;
'You are mine,' it sings; 'my love, my joy,
though not fenced in by bone and sinew,
yet clothed with flesh. Come fly with
me!'

Let them see it, these you have called to
care for me: let them see my soul, let
them hear your song, let them glory in
salvation, let them even see the valley of
Baca become a place of springs! – if pass
through suffering I must.

For I am lifted on heavenly wings, and
whether I will be healed or not I shall
rejoice. Rejoice, my soul! Yet will I rejoice
in the Lord!

I lift you who carry me, professionally;
   be blessed.
May peace come to you, may soul
   richness be yours.
May Christ touch you, call you, lead you,
   consecrate you, save you.
May you be caught up in the dance of
   eternity.
May joy be yours.
And whatever may befall me, may we
   meet again in Christ's embrace one day.
I bless you in Christ's name.

RECOVERY

> *'I praise you, Lord, because you have*
> *saved me and kept my enemies from*
> *gloating over me.*
> *I cried to you for help, O Lord my God, and*
> *you healed me; you kept me from the grave,*
> *you restored my life . . . '*

Psalm 30.1–3 GNB

No duty is more
urgent than that
of returning
thanks.
St Ambrose

A day dawns when you feel better; not
completely better, but better than before.

Maybe it was a more restful night;

maybe the pain seems to have gone;

maybe bits and pieces are working
again;

maybe breakfast looks more
interesting;

maybe you can't put your
finger on it, but

you feel as if you can look
forward to the rest of the day.

In hope we count on the possibilities of the future and we do not remain imprisoned in the institutions of the past.
Jürgen Moltmann

It is not so much being a bit further on the road, but that you've turned a corner. You can begin to hope; and the future looks brighter. Gradually the memories recede: the memories of how wretched it felt, the insidiousness of the fear, the discomfort, the helplessness of being so weak, the stab of a sudden pain. Yes, it's a relief to turn one's back on all that.

Hope is hearing the melody of the future. Faith is to dance to it.
Rubem Alves

There comes a moment when I realise I am not so much being carried by him as walking with him again. The faithfulness and goodness of God are real and working. Confidence is returning; so is the desire to praise. The words of the medieval mystic Julian, 'All shall be well . . . ', carry weight again. I need to put my thankfulness to God into words: thankfulness for the way my heavy weariness and burdens are being replaced by peace of heart and ease for the body.

RECOVERY

With all my soul I praise you, my Lord!

*From the bottom of my heart I praise your
holy name!*

*Dear Lord,
let me never forget how kind you are:*

may your love be planted deep in my soul.

*I am filled with thanksgiving to you, Lord,
for I feel the reality of your loving
forgiveness,*

and know you are healing all my disease.

As you fill my life with good things,

blessing me with your love and mercy,

I rejoice in you,
and offer myself anew in your service,
trusting in the strength of Jesus.

Amen

Inspired by Psalm 103

CONVALESCENCE

*It is of the Lord's mercies that we are not
consumed, because his compassions fail not.
They are new every morning;
great is thy faithfulness.*

Lamentations 3:22–23 AV

*Suffering is a
cleansing fire that
clears away
triviality and
restlessness.*
Louis E. Bisch

Today we think of recovery, and the pathway to it – convalescence.

Convalescence – the very word means 'to get well'.

Yet we can convalesce in different ways, at different levels.

Our convalescence may be as simple as healing after an operation (yet God is our healer there); it may be moving on through bitterness of soul (and God is our healer there, too).

So it is even possible to convalesce when some signs of our illness remain, because healing relates to more than our bodies, it extends to soul and spirit too.

The man who has
not tasted the
bitter does not
know what the
sweet is.
Jewish proverb

Convalescence is a moving on. You have been long enough in this place: time to move on.

Illness initially focuses our attention on ourselves. By God's grace, we then focus on him, particularly if our illness threatens our very being.

In convalescence, we start to orientate to others again, to pick up the burden of their existence, to allow our hearts to beat for them, to find ways of loving and praying for them.

In illness, it is 'us and God'.

In wellness it is 'them and God'.
Convalescence is the bridge.

Blessed Lord, you who from the cross itself
declared 'Behold, your mother!
Behold your son!', so help me to focus
my being on you and others – today.
May I be a channel of blessings to others
from now on. May I be a channel of
blessings and find wellness in a myriad
of little ways, by your grace.

CONVALESCENCE

*And this is the confidence which we have
in him, that if we ask anything according to
his will he hears us.*

1 John 5.14 RSV

Blessed Lord, it is so good to be making progress. From deep in my heart I thank you that I can feel more able to be me. Remembering how bad things were, how awful I felt, I just praise you, Lord, for all that has been done, and what has happened to bring me to this convalescent stage. I know your hand has been over me, and your touch has sustained me.

Blessed Lord, now I can say I want to go forward again with you. I pray you: Bless me with the motivation, the strength and the means to move on. With the nudging and leading of your Holy Spirit may I know where and how to answer your calling to me.

Blessed Lord, I dedicate myself again to your service: give me grace, I pray, to obey your words; give me the vision, I pray, to grasp again the opportunities of relating and serving. Open my heart, open my ears and eyes, I pray, to share again the worship and service, prayers and praises of your faithful people.

Blessed Lord, you have been so good to me: I know and feel your blessings over and above what earthly medicines and mercies bring. In many little ways may I, in my turn, be used to bring signs of blessing and of well-being to others in need.

In Jesus' name, I thank you and trust you in all these things. Amen

ADAPTING TO A NEW WAY OF LIFE

When you are old, you will stretch out your hands, and another will gird you and carry you where you do not wish to go.

John 21.18 RSV

The wise adapt themselves to circumstances, as water moulds itself to the pitcher.
Confucius

We hate the very thought of this change that Jesus predicts for Peter.

It had a specific meaning for him; but it has general meaning for the majority of us.

So many people cannot do things. Some can't talk. Think of that. Some cannot walk, or see, or hear. And some need help with all sorts of things I'd rather not have help with.

How often did I thank God that I could do those things? Very rarely.

And now that which I feared – it is here.

I must adapt. God is revealing to me new things about myself as I am being forced to adapt.

The wind blows on me from a new direction. It is for me to adjust the sails.

It is misleading to imagine that we are developed in spite of our circumstances. We are developed because of them. It is not mastery in the circumstances that is needed; it is mastery over them.

Oswald Chambers

The harder the wind blows, the faster the progress I can make. It may not be in the direction that I had intended. But all too often our directions are the wrong ones; the Lord knows better than we. Too often it is as Ogden Nash said: 'Gentlemen, we are making excellent progress, but we are headed in the wrong direction.'

God calls us to master the circumstance, to maintain heart peace in it, to continue to praise him and seek not to complain: and in our weakness we are forced to cry out to him for grace, for peace, and for forgiveness.

In fitness, I found circumstances to overcome.
They came on mountains, in seas, in challenges of all sorts.
But now I face the biggest of them all, and I do not have to step out of the house; God grant me mastery over this circumstance by his grace.

ADAPTING TO A NEW
WAY OF LIFE

From glory to glory advancing, we praise thee,
O Lord;
Thy name with the Father and Spirit be ever adored.

Liturgy of St James, trans. Charles Humphreys

Before all our prayer, may our praises rise to you, O Lord; because of your love and faithfulness we can depend on you. Though you are unchanging in your holiness and steadfast righteousness, yet you continually give us dependable promises of your redemptive acts. We trust you to transform our situations, our lives and our world.

In Christ you were transfigured before your faithful people, though they found it hard to grasp the reality; so we trust you to adapt us to experience the signs of your glory and victory, even in those moments when all seems cloudy or confused.

Thanksgiving, and glory and worship, and blessing and love,
One heart and one song have the saints upon earth and above.

Lord, my heart is so thankful you made me able to learn new ways and to adapt:
– to solid food – to walking and talking –
to working and adult life
– to responsibility and the care of little ones –
to a slower pace
– to think first, recall experience and value wisdom.

Lord, my heart is so thankful you made me
flexible, enabling me:
– to accept your gift of faith – to make changes
in attitude
– to adjust my lifestyle – to grow into new
relationships
– to be more forgiving – to change harmful habits.

*From strength unto strength we go forward on Sion's
highway,*
To appear before God in the city of infinite day.

Merciful Lord, I nevertheless have to confess:
– to becoming less flexible as the years pass by
– to resisting coming to terms with some changes
– to turning my face sometimes from difficult
challenges.

*Lord, have mercy, Christ, have mercy, Lord have
mercy.*

By your most Holy Spirit grant me now,
I pray:
– your comfort when I grieve lost abilities
– your wisdom to discern changed limitations
– your good counsel in trying new ways to cope.

By your most Holy Spirit may I be enabled with
grace, I pray:
– to accept what on the face of it is
unacceptable
– to work on coming to terms with restrictions of
body or soul
– to adapt my days to serving you in new ways.

*Evermore, O Lord, to thy servants thy presence be
nigh;*
Ever fit us by service on earth for thy service on high.

HEALING

Go and tell what you have seen and heard:
the blind see, the lame walk,
lepers are cleansed, the deaf hear,
the dead are raised to life,
and good news is proclaimed to the poor.

Luke 7.22 FJV

Healing is the
restoration of the
possibility of ful-
filling the purpose
for which you
were created.
A.C.Oomen

Healing was a central part of Jesus'
ministry.
We believe he calls his people to heal in
his name today.
What is healing?
When we want to be healed we want to
be freed from disease, distress and pain;
rightly so.
The curing of symptoms achieves that.

If healing means more than relief of
symptoms, how do we define or describe
it? To put it positively, is it so that I may
enjoy life, unrestricted by illness or
injury? But can I do that all on my own,
just by myself, for myself alone? With
whom, for whom is my life to be lived?

No healing was ever designed to take you back to where you were but to move you on into new adventures with God, of healing our relationship with him, with each other, with ourselves and with the community of which we are members.
Russ Parker

As well as the body and soul of an individual, healing involves relationships: Especially with those who give us life, and with whom we share life. That sounds like family; but the creative power that causes our life comes, we believe , not by accident or human love but ultimately through the design of God. My life – my being – is a gift of God. For what?

When we know healing is happening let us ask, 'For what new purpose is God blessing me this way?' Living for him gives meaning to our lives, and leads to the fulfilment of all things.

Healing means becoming more and more the person he has always meant me – and you – to be, at this time. Whenever we are hindered in this by sickness, sorrow or other suffering, we rightly pray for the living Christ to meet us at the point of our need to bring release and redemption. Yet when we feel his restoring touch it will not only bring the balm of peace, it will bring a call and a challenge to live in the ways of his Kingdom.

HEALING

Lord, here I am, in your presence, in my
need of healing.
Forgive me for when I have thought of
healing in a self-centred way.
Yes, I *do* want to be free of illness,
    I *do* want to be able to enjoy my life
      unrestricted, unfettered.
Yet I know you have a plan for me, and it
involves more than doing something for
you.
It involves being something with you.
And I know, in my heart of hearts, that I
have often longed for a deeper relationship with you, my Father;
that I might know your love for me, your
child;
and in that love I might be released into
your service in a new way –
the way of the beloved.

I love to serve you
I live to serve you
I thrill to hear you
to feel your presence
to know your help.
So I pray boldly – bring me release
                    – bring me redemption
                    – bring me healing.
But do it, my Lord and King, that I might
plumb the depths of service for you
and reach the heights of fellowship with
    you,
for there my heart is.

Heal me and make me whole
  heal me and make me whole
    heal me and make me whole
O lover of my soul.

PRAYER FOR OTHERS
WHO SUFFER

*Rejoice always, pray constantly, give thanks
in all circumstances; for this is the will of
God in Christ Jesus for you.*

1 Thessalonians 5.16–18 RSV

*Hezekiah took his
morning mail,
with its bad news,
and forwarded it
to God.*
William Vander
Hoven, on 2 Kings
19.14

News of great need keeps flooding in.
Through the media come accounts of
conflict, of folk in pain or terror, great
distress or sorrow.

How can I identify with little ones so far
away when I find it so hard to see what a
friend with cancer is really going
through? And what can I do to help?   I
feel so useless. Perhaps that's why, when
face to face with someone in the valley of
the shadow, what I say can sound so
shallow, pious or just plain crass.

Perhaps I should first listen; but it isn't
the easy way out. It can lead to identifica-
tion: sharing the pain, the fear, and feeling the isolation of the sufferer. But

where do I go with that agony and desperation? I don't want to dump *my* distress back on the one in need!

Who listens to us when we feel the pains and fears of others ? How do we express the need that is plucking at our own heartstrings? Is there any other place to lay those prayers than at the foot of the cross, where the one who always listens burns away the sickness, sorrow and sin of this world? He knows before we speak what it is all about. He is the one by whose wounds they, and we, are healed.

Bringing helpless loved ones to Jesus was never a light job: some carried a friend on a stretcher up an outside staircase, broke through the roof – with people underneath, for goodness sake! And perfect goodness, incarnate, spoke with authority to bring wholeness of soul and body. Christ in his risen power hears every prayer, spoken or acted out, and recognising even our mustard-seed-sized faith gives his answer to us when we lay at his feet the ones whose agony we feel.

PRAYER FOR OTHERS
WHO SUFFER

My Lord, here I stand before you
aware of so many needs, so much
suffering.
I know that my prayers are as incense
rising before your throne –
and I am heartened and encouraged.
You know all things: there is not
a thought, no inspiration
that is not already known to you.
So I can't inspire you, nor remind you,
nor teach you;
I am but a child.
But you give me the right to talk with
you
and to ask of you, because I am a child –
your child.
And so I lift this one, so on my heart,
before you.

You know.
Show mercy, O Lord!
Draw close, O Lord!
Encourage and heal and bless,
I pray.
And that one!   I lift them to you.
I cannot do a thing –
Except this. I lift that one to you in my
love.
Yes, your love is greater.
Let your ways be established in
that one's life.
Draw that one close . . .
close . . . in heavenly embrace.
And the world?
Yes, some parts are on my heart.
So much suffering, so much pain.
I lay them all at the foot of
the cross
and I lay my perplexity and
anguish there, too,
and I say if I am to help relieve
any poverty, any sickness
tell me what to do:
I am willing.
And I will listen.

WHOLENESS

May the God of peace himself
sanctify you wholly;
and may your spirit and soul and body be
kept sound and blameless at the coming of
our Lord Jesus Christ.

1 Thessalonians 5.23 RSV

When we use the word 'wholeness' what do we mean: more than healthiness perhaps?

This is the Gospel . . . that God is at work in the world not only creating it with a purpose of wholeness and perfection, but working to overcome all the evil . . . to redeem the world . . . and to heal all sickness and disease . . .   Fr Jim Wilson

As we look for pointers to help us understand and seek wholeness we realise other people, and our relationships, must be involved, as well as the integration of our own spirit, mind and body.

Health is a concept which cannot be defined. To define it is to kill it. Nor can it be possessed. It can only be shared.

Revd Dr Michael Wilson

Wholeness: a growing awareness of harmony between oneself, one's neighbours, one's environment and God.

A Time to Heal, Report for the House of Bishops

Wholeness is a perfection of relationships such that to be me I have to be me in such a way that I help you to be the you that you are meant to be.

Bishop David Jenkins

For the process to be fulfilled, surely the frailties of our humanity cannot be overlooked.

Health is a matter of wholeness and not perfection. Health has to do with being real and offering our sins, mistakes and brokenness as multicoloured threads to be woven into a rich tapestry of humanity by the healing grace of God.

Robert Raines

St Paul saw this as a mystery, predicting that we Christians shall all be changed.

Wholeness does not consist in removing a present source of travail; it demands a complete transformation of the person's attitude to life, which in turn is an outward sign of a transfigured personality.

Revd Dr Martin Israel

Then we shall be alert to the sound of God, and desire to become as he is.

Health is being in tune with the song the Creator is eternally singing.

Dean Sydney Evans

Reflecting on Luke 2.52, Bishop Morris sees Christ's growth: mentally, physically, spiritually and socially as essential areas for perfect health.

It is in the lives of the saints that we see the process of this coming to wholeness most clearly, that alone prepares man for the gift and goal of holiness that God wills for him.   Bishop Morris Maddocks

When wholeness comes in these four areas, there is holiness indeed. Holiness is the goal and Jesus has revealed that holiness in all its perfection.

Bishop Morris Maddocks

It sounds as though wholeness is not so much a state as a process, a journey, an adventure, evolving interactively.

. . . recovering the full proclamation of the Good News, that salvation is for the whole person and that Jesus came to bring us the fullness of life in every possible dimension . . . returning to the biblical view of man, God's view of man: that holiness is wholeness.   Francis Macnutt

WHOLENESS

Lord, I am fragmented.
> Please make me whole.

Lord, there are parts of me that I don't like
and there are parts that I do.
Yet I am the sum of them.
> Please make me whole.

Lord, I have gifts of creativity, emotion
   and logic;
> Integrate my being, and make me
> whole, dear Lord.

Lord, I am spirit, soul and body
and some of it is broken.

Dear, dear Lord: I cry to you to
   make me whole.
Mend me and integrate me afresh.
Things have got corrupted:
   re-program me, O Lord,
That I might be the human being
   you always wanted me to be.

Dear Lord, I am spirit, soul and body
and I am not in balance.
Tune me so that I might harmonise
with your Holy Spirit,
that he might lead me in all truth.
Help me hear the music of heaven,
the songs of the angels;
the whisper of your command,
and grant me strength in soul and
body to obey.

And dear Lord, I am one, just one,
of your Church on earth.
You called it your Body: you called it
your Temple, with us as living stones.
Grant that I might be truly a part, truly a
living stone
with a function, with a purpose,
giving and receiving
loving and caring
being loved and cared for
doing your will.

My Lord, I offer you all of me.
Make me beautiful,
make me whole, O Lord, I pray.

SETBACKS

We are afflicted in every way, but not crushed; perplexed, but not driven to despair; persecuted, but not forsaken; struck down, but not destroyed;
always carrying in the body the death of Jesus,
so that the life of Jesus may also be manifested in our bodies.

2 Corinthians 4.8–10 RSV

Each one of us has our own cycle of growth which brings with it ups and downs, summers and winters, good times and bad times; setbacks and times of drought are part of life. They are phases we have to go through and a new start is always possible.
Jean Vanier

Insurance adverts include the words, 'Please remember that the value of your investment can fall as well as rise'. For years we have been encouraged by the ads hardly to believe such safety warnings; but the recent movements of the stock market mean few can be unaware of such setbacks. They are a reality.

Should doctors and hospitals have safety disclaimers? What would we feel if on the brass plate at the surgery it said, 'Patients can get worse, as well as better'? What if there was a big sign at the hospital entrance, 'People can deteriorate as well as improve'? It is the reality. We don't want to believe it, for it is discomforting.

Setbacks happen. They can be more or less expected, or totally unexpected. Shock or disappointment are likely first reactions, together with fear or anger. We may find ourselves led into theological wrestlings, such as Rabbi Kushner details in his book. We might try to tackle the setbacks with stoicism, but does that really for work for us? What does it all mean? Can we set what is happening in a wider context?

What resources do we have to meet the challenge? What resilience and inward strength have we available? Who will stand by us?
Where are you, O Lord, in all this? If we are relating to God, even by making complaint, let us pray we stay in contact.

Hang on, even while the prayer for help seems unanswered. Trust that he will not let a loved child slip out of his grasp. Can we live ready to take whatever may be offered to redeem the setbacks? It may not at first seem obvious, and it can be hard to believe that God's grace is sufficient, as Paul writes, and that his power really can be made perfect in my weaknesses.

SETBACKS

Lord, my heart is not haughty,
nor my eyes lofty.
Neither do I concern myself with great
matters,
nor with things too profound for me.
Surely I have calmed and quieted my soul,
like a weaned child with his mother;
like a weaned child is my soul within me.

Psalm 131 1–2 RAV

Why, O Lord?

I think of it as a change of fortunes; perhaps, if I am honest, a mistake on the part of the doctor.

But as I harbour such thoughts, a worm eats at my insides, and my life ebbs away.

I have settled that you are in charge, and I choose to stand on that solid ground; I may not understand, but there is much that is too great for me, that I do not understand.

Lord, grant me faith to believe in your goodness. Even when the setbacks come.

Lord, help me to see the redeeming elements of this setback, that in my weakness, my vulnerability, I might find your power.

Dear Lord, help me to know you afresh, that my fear might be relieved, for it rises in front of me, and Satan has painted a big notice for me saying 'Defeat – it is defeat'. He shows it to me often.

My Lord, be like water on a hot rock: let the reality of your presence rise up like steam, let it surround me, suffuse me. Let me see you and naught beside: hold me, hold me, hold me.

And I will praise you; and my praise will rise up like incense before you, and you will come to me.

And whisper your words to my poor soul because I choose to trust in you.
I might die (Satan says);
      I am alive
           I am alive
                  I am alive
And shall glorify you for ever and ever.
      Amen

SHOCK

My God, my God, why have you forsaken me?

*Life is not as
idle ore
But iron dug
from central
gloom
And heated hot
with burning
fears
And dipped in
baths with
hissing tears,
And battered
with the shocks
of doom
To shape and
use.*
Alfred, Lord
Tennyson

When our capacity to adjust is temporarily overwhelmed, we become disabled for a time: we can do nothing. We cannot believe this has happened: we are in a state of shock.

There was a fateful day in 2001, on September 11th, when a calamity too enormous to comprehend unfolded before our eyes. Television cameras beamed the scenes into our living rooms: we watched the faces of eyewitnesses as the passenger planes ploughed into the World Trade Center. We watched as people launched themselves out of the building to certain death rather than be engulfed by flames. We watched the shock in the lives of eyewitnesses. No-one could continue with life. The pause button was pressed.

*Lord, it is dark!
Lord, are you
there in the darkness? Where are
you, Lord? Do
you love me still?
I haven't wearied
you? Lord,
answer me!
Answer! It is
so dark!*
Michael Quoist

And so it is when great and unexpected change directly affects *us* for the worse. Running adjustments we make without difficulty. But seismic shifts in our direction: that is a different matter!

Then we cry out to God. In our darkness, in our lostness, in our littleness, we need light, and reassurance, and a rock. It is so

I would say to my soul, O my soul, this is not the place of despair; this is not the time to despair in. As long as mine eyes can find a promise in the Bible, as long as there is a moment left me of breath, or life in this world, so long will I wait or look for mercy, so long will I fight against unbelief and despair.
John Bunyan

hard for us to comprehend that sin's sway is yet so powerful. Tragedy, and tears, mourning and weeping, death and dying – all so much a part of human experience.

More difficult still is the shocking reality of the deep hatred of man for man: how *can* the Cambodian killing fields truly have been a reality? How *can* the Holocaust have happened?

And so we need the Rock. In doubt we cry, 'The Lord reigns!' – and we come to realise that we are caught up in the same human condition much more closely than we had thought.

Weeping and grief, dying and death, vying and fighting, war and hatred – all can touch us with their greasy finger and we recoil: but the stain remains. This is an 'us' thing, not a 'them' thing, and crises teach us so. We pray as people touched by these things.

Yet in the doubt and the shock we become stronger, if we will but believe, if we will but accept that we are God's children; if we will but respond with Dostoyevski, and confess, 'It is not as a child that I believe and confess Jesus Christ. My "hosanna" is born of a furnace of doubt.' Sometimes it is so for us, and dogged perseverance draws us through, together with deep encouragement from those of our friends who have also suffered.

SHOCK

Why, why, why
  when all was well,
    when you gave me no hint of such
    a change of fortune,
      when I relaxed into you,
        did you turn my light off
          and, like an earthquake, tip
          my life over?

Lord, it is dark!
Lord, are you
there in the dark-
ness? Where are
you, Lord?
Michael Quoist

I am disorientated, afraid – so afraid! –
and bruised and broken. Just like that.
It happened just like that.

My Lord, I know your love. I have lived
in the knowledge of it these past many
years.

My Lord, I have felt your hand on my
  shoulder, your love in my life.
Help me now, for I feel that my
  Gethsemane has come
and yet I have no assurance of its
  purpose
for I cannot see.

And I ask myself: what is reality?
　All that I leant upon has gone
　　and joy has turned into tears and grief.
　　Job is my comforter.

I cry to you: be my reality!
　I cry to you: though all else fails,
　　be true to me.
　　　I cry to you: O God of the universe,
　　　maker and sustainer,
　　　　if you are in love with my soul
　　　　I need you close
　　　　　for I have nowhere to
　　　　　rest my head.

Lord Jesus Christ,　You did not promise me that, I know.
have mercy on　And I have had tribulation;
me, a sinner.　you did promise me that, I know.
The Jesus Prayer

My Lord, I have inherited your promises:
now grant me all of them.

'Peace I leave with you' – you said –
　'my peace I give unto you' –
you said: so be my reality, be my peace,
　be my strong tower.
For I have no hope but you.
Help me rest in you. I want to rest in you.
I rest in you.

ANXIETY

> *How precious is your loving kindness, O*
> *God! Therefore the children of men put their*
> *trust under the shadow of your wings . . . for*
> *with you is the fountain of light. In your*
> *light do we see light.*

Psalm 36.7–9 RAV

Lord Jesus make
my heart sit
down.
African proverb

When I look toward my problem, I see . . .
what do I see? I see confusing shapes in
turmoil: it is like a battle in the mist, and
I can see neither victor nor vanquished. I
can only nurse an uneasy feeling that I
am the vanquished. My faith takes flight
in precise proportion to my anxiety and
fear.

Anatole Broyard said that fear is like a
catheter inserted into the soul, draining
away its life. Certainly it robs me of
strength for today; and helps tomorrow
not one jot. Deliver me . . .

But who is this? A radiant Man, who bursts upon the scene and proclaims to me. 'Do not fear: it is your Father's good pleasure to give you the Kingdom! Sell what you have – give alms – provide for yourself a lasting treasure in the heavens – for where your treasure is, your heart is also.'

I am in two worlds. God grant me his light in my night! And strength to grasp his hand, and salve for my eyes, that I might see his Kingdom – given to me. And grant me courage and faith that I may not fear to step toward this gift. For I find anxiety and fear take flight in precise proportion to my faith. Be thou my vision, O Lord of my heart! Burst in and be my guide, my light, my all.

Drop Thy still dew of quietness
Till all our strivings cease;
Take from our souls the strain and stress
And let our ordered lives confess
The beauty of Thy peace.

J. G. Whittier

ANXIETY

Why art thou so cast down, O my soul?
and why art thou disquieted within me?
Hope in God:
for I shall yet praise him, who is the health
of my countenance, and my God.

Psalm 42.5, 42.11, 43.5 AV

It is evening Lord; I nearly said, 'Good evening, Lord.'
But I am not too sure it is a good evening.

In fact the doors are shut where I am, and I remember that one evening your disciples had the doors shut – for fear, even when there was nothing to fear.

Lord, I confess I've got my doors shut tonight; the ordinary house doors of course, for burglaries do happen round here. Is it common sense or fear to lock those doors?

But I've got other doors that feel locked – sometimes my heart feels locked into anxiety, and there is no simple key to undo it. Lord what is the answer?

What do I really need from you tonight, Lord, deep down in my soul?

Lord, I recall that, when they were locked in, you came and said, 'Peace be with you.' Then they were glad, and with good reason, for they experienced your living presence.

Grant me, and all who are overcome with fear, to know your real presence, to receive the peace that passes all understanding, to be secure from feverish agitations, to be serene this night.

Lord, like the Psalmist I cry, not knowing why I am so disquieted. I would love to hope as he commends, to be able to praise you: the health of my countenance.

In the midst of the doubts and dreads grant us, Lord, hope that becomes the courage to overcome dark nights in the soul, so that we are not anxious for tomorrow.

Lord, through your beloved disciple John I've heard that perfect love casts out fear. There are very many of us who need the embrace of your perfect love right now.

As you let the fullness of your love rest in our souls, trustworthy Lord, I thank you that the light of your glory drives away darkness, and fills us with your peace, your hope and your blessing. Amen

FRUSTRATION

The Lord, the God of their fathers, sent word to them through his mesengers again and again . . . but they mocked God's messengers, despised his words and scoffed at his prophets . . .
2 Chronicles
36.15, 16 NIV

Frustration is born out of helplessness. We plan, we move to execute our plans – and something happens to render our intentions impossible. Of course, this is the reality of life, and we learn to live with it. We note those who do not, whose early temper tantrums develop into sour teenage rebellion unchecked, only to progress to aggressive adult ego-centricity and mellow inevitably into crabbed old age. We note them, and we determine not to become like them.

But there is a great test before us now. In illness, we plan – and a multitude of problems harass us into helplessness. That planned holiday – rudely inter-rupted by a required admission. The trip to see the family, hijacked by difficult symptoms. So many people – caring, professional people – all coming to my door: the day a procession of well-mean-ing visitors, so that quiet thought, and order, is no longer possible. And when

*When the
frustration of
my helplessness
seemed greatest,
I discovered God's
grace was more
than sufficient . . .
and after my
imprisonment I
could look back
and see how God
used my powerless-
ness for his
purpose.
What he has
chosen for my
most signficant
witness was not
my triumphs or
victories . . . but
my defeat.*
Charles Colson

that trip actually does happen, further frustrations! We cannot do what we thought we could. 'Everything conspires against me! I am helpless . . . '

Frustration colours the universe. We frustrate one another. Satan frustrates us. We frustrate God. God frustrates us! How can we lay down the particular burden of frustration? Stop it developing into bitterness and anger? There is an 'I want' about frustration. God frustrates us when he knows better than we, as we frustrate our children when we know better. We frustrate one another to achieve our own ends, when there is a conflict of desires. Satan will always seek to frustrate the Spirit-led man or woman, whilst being most accommodating to the rebel against God.

But God knows it all. Though even he is frustrated by our free will, yet he is the victor. It will become apparent. Then can we link our longings with his? Can we bear our limitations for him? May we also be the victor at the end?

There is glory here, May I bring my frustrations, my defeats, to the foot of the cross – that greatest symbol of frustration and victory? May I? God grant me grace so to do!

19 FRUSTRATION

*Hear my prayer, O God; don't turn away
from my plea!
I am gripped by fear and trembling; I am
overcome with horror.
I wish I had wings like a dove. I would fly
away and find rest.
I would fly far away and make my home
in the desert.*

Psalm 55.1, 5–7 GNB

Like your Psalmist I pray, good Lord:
I am gripped and I cannot get free . . . ,
I wish, but I have not . . . , I would fly . . .
I would fly, but I cannot . . .; Like him, I
pray: If it were . . . If it were, I could . . . ;
But it is not, and Lord, I cannot; I am
hemmed in by unmet needs, wishes and
many a wistful, 'If only . . . '

Good Lord God, I have to confess that
sometimes the trouble is:
– my need to be in control of my life
Lord, have mercy
– my obstinate refusal of help and grace
Christ, have mercy
– my unrealistic belief in fantasy solutions
Lord, have mercy

Good Lord God, in the midst of disease
and feeling helpless, and remembering

I will put my trust in your steadfast love; my heart will rejoice in your salvation. I will sing to you, my Lord, for you have dealt so bountifully with me.
Psalm 13.5, 6 CW

your promise to set free the oppressed, we pray for your deliverance:

– when every move seems checked; there is no space to take control; and our decisions have slipped out of our hands
Good Lord, deliver us

– when impotence, any sort of impotence, disables us; or incontinence, any sort of incontinence, gnaws at the innards; or being thwarted leads to growlings in the guts *Good Lord, deliver us*

– when frustration is the shape of the cross for today; and banging on the very gates of heaven feels a fruitless exercise; and being unheard we seethe in our souls *Good Lord, deliver us*

Good Lord God, as we look to you, as we call to you, as we wait for you, as we wait some more for you, eventually we have to give in to you in the only place we can be absolutely sure to find you: the cross.

– Where even you felt forsaken, yet were able to speak the words of forgiveness, promise and homely care; speak also to us. *Hear us, good Lord*

– Where you were lifted up from the earth, to draw all, even us, to yourself; that you may grant us salvation, which is the space and liberty to become the people you mean us to be.
Hear us, good Lord

ANGER

*Be angry but do not sin; do not let
the sun go down on your anger, and give
no opportunity to the devil.*

Ephesians 4.26–27 RSV

Anger happens. It is very common. It comes upon people like us – it rears its ugly head – can erupt fiercely – feels both furious and frustrating – can get out of control. When it causes us to say or do things we regret we feel bad.

Feelings happen. Feelings are morally neutral. Physical feelings, like hunger, happen to us and indicate a bodily need.

Emotional feelings like anger indicate unmet personal needs for acceptance, belonging, a good self image and space in which to make decisions. When needs like these are thwarted uncomfortable feelings like anger, fear and sorrow arise.

Anger arises, and is morally neutral, though the situations and actions that cause it may be wrong, unjust, abusive or oppressive. The responses we make when we feel angry may be morally right or wrong. We should respond for there is a

Anger is a message, a revelation . . . If we are attempting to hear God's word, we must listen to anger as carefully as we listen to joy, peace, fear and fatigue.
Kathleen Fischer

Anger denied subverts community. Anger expressed directly is a mode of taking the other seriously, of caring.
Beverly Harrison

danger of an anger which 'settles into a biting resentment and slowly paralyses a generous heart', as Henri Nouwen writes in *The Way of the Heart*. But how do we respond to the feeling of anger?

If we don't face it, accepting its reality, we will probably deny it, whether directly or implicitly. Denial only hides anger: it will return in unexpected ways to get us down and depress us.

Far better, humanly speaking, is to identify, understand, and express the feelings, acknowledging the effect they have, both on us and others. At this point we begin to identify our unmet emotional needs. It can be liberating to decide to take some responsibility for meeting those needs, and seek to meet them by making or refreshing effective relationships. These can be relationships with others or with God.

Within our personal relationships there is a way to express our anger appropriately; but it is the way of humility and openness. It accepts the need to look at issues from another perspective. It marries honesty and love, and coats it all in a genuine desire for growth, change and relationship. It requires grace and forgiveness.

ANGER

*My God, my God, look upon me; Why hast
thou forsaken me: and art so far from my
health, and from the words of my
complaint?
O my God, I cry in the daytime, but thou
hearest not: and in the night season also I
take no rest.*

Psalm 22.1–2 BCP

My God, that just about sums it up. My
God, like the Psalmist I have a complaint. Did you not know? Did you not
care? Like the Psalmist I asked: How long
will you overlook me? Why are you not
there when I need you?

At first, dear Lord (hear the sarcasm in my
tone), I was merely simmering; the irrita-
tion had been festering in my soul, and I
was coming up to the boil. Now, I am
frustrated, indignant, vexed almost
beyond measure, boiling away about the
injustice of it all.

*I will cry unto God with my voice: even unto
God will I cry with my voice, and he shall
hearken unto me.
Will you absent yourself for ever: and will
you be no more entreated?
Have you forgotten to be gracious: will you
shut up your loving kindness in displeasure?*

Psalm 77.1, 7, 9 BCP

Thy rebuke hath broken my heart; I am full of heaviness.
Psalm 69.21 BCP

My God, I have to say it feels worse than just not being cared about. Through gritted teeth I plead: Why should you be so angry with me? What have I done that was so bad, so awful. I feel so hurt – even by you.

My God, I have to say, like the Psalmist: I had hoped for sympathy, but there was none; for comfort, but I found none. Even in the midst of all this, when I feel so constrained, yet I must lodge my complaint – register my distress with you.

O let thine ears consider well the voice of my complaint.
Psalm 130.2 BCP

My God, it is not comfortable to pour out all this anger; I am sorry I seem to be so rough with you, yet it does seem to help. My God, in reality I know you have every right to be angry with me; as the Psalmist says: If you kept a record of our sins, who could escape being condemned? Yes, I do believe you listen to my rantings; through Jesus you understand how we feel, and accept us when we share it.

As William Blake put it:
   I was angry with my friend;
   I told my wrath, my wrath did end.
   I was angry with my foe;
   I told it not, my wrath did grow.

I pray you, in Jesus' name: Be my friend, deliver me from my resentments, and let my wrath come to an end. Thank you; my God, you are so wonderful! Amen.

LOSS

If anyone's work is burnt up,
then he will lose it;
but he himself will be saved,
as if he had escaped through the fire.

1 Corinthians 3.15 GNB

No one ever told
me that grief is so
like fear.
C. S. Lewis

In the Easter season of 2002 the papers and the TV were full of the story of the life, death and funeral of the Queen Mother. It seemed as though most of a nation felt grief to some extent; and wanted to offer sympathy to those in the Royal Family who suffered the loss most keenly. It is the heartache of being bereaved of someone close and dear that strikes us hardest, filling us with the deepest sorrow.

In times of privation and sickness there are other losses. At first sight they may not seem so important, yet real they are and need to be faced and lived through. To lose a limb, an organ or some other part of the physical body is real loss. We are shocked by it and find it hard to believe. What I see in the mirror reflects what I feel in my soul: mourning part of my self-image questions my identity, in many ways.

*Jesus said,
'Blessed are those
who mourn, for
they shall be
comforted'.*

It may be:
• strength, vitality, virility that are threatened . . .
• my ability, my mobility, my independence that is going, going . . .
• loss of my role in the family, my purpose, what gives meaning in life . . .
• losing the powers of easy breathing, speaking, hearing, seeing . . .
• the absence of friends, a prayer partner, a dear pet . . .
• losing my contact with God, the surety of faith or of spiritual reality . . .
• the impending loss of earthly life . . .

*Grief is itself a
medicine.*
William Cowper

In all these we can suffer, to greater or lesser extent, the feelings we know only too well in personal grief: the waves of sorrow, the searching and yearning, the anger, the guilt, the questioning, emptiness, and darkness. All these, and more, are normal. To acknowledge, face, express and share them safely is all rightly part of our mourning.

Denial closes us to the possibility of comfort. Only when we engage in our needful grieving are we open to receive consolation and strength. When our hearts are opened and our tears flow we are ready for the Comforter. Just as we usually learn more from mistakes than successes, so we can grow more through our losses than our gains.

LOSS

He was despised and rejected by men;
a man of sorrows and acquainted with
grief:
and as one from whom folk hid their faces
he was despised, and we esteemed him not.
Surely he has borne our griefs and carried
our sorrows.

Isaiah 53.3–4a RSV

Lord, I confess I find it hard to believe,
to believe you really understand about
sorrow and loss.
You see, dear Lord, I'm so full up about
what's going on,
so full up about what I'm missing.

Lord, I confess it sounds self-centred,
but the pain of my grief is gnawing at
the soft centre of my soul.
That's why I find it so hard to listen to
what you say,
to pay attention to your presence in
your Word.

Can it really be true you are acquainted
with my sorrow?
That you truly understand the depth of
my feelings of loss?
Can you really carry some of the weight
of my desolation?
You see, Lord, my soul is very sorrowful.

Then Jesus said to Peter, James and John,
  'My soul is very sorrowful, even to death;
  remain here and watch with me.'
And going a little farther he fell on his face,
  and prayed,
  'My Father, if it be possible, let this cup
  pass from me;
  nevertheless, not as I will, but as thou
  wilt.'   Matthew 26.38–39 RSV

Yes, Lord; of course you know; you've
  been through it yourself.
  You know just what it's like, grief-
  stricken on your own,
in the middle of the night when
  everything seems to be closing in;
  you know – you understand – you care.

In your great compassion, dear Lord, let
  there be somebody,
  somebody to listen and comfort me
  when all feels lost.
Lord, I do trust you – really I do – even
  though sometimes,
  sometimes things can be so heavy, you
  know – you know.

Thank you, Lord, for being there, hearing
  my prayer, and lifting my head,
  lifting my voice to want to praise you:
  despite all that's gone.

And the ransomed of the Lord shall return,
  and come with singing to Zion;
everlasting joy shall be upon their heads;
  they shall obtain joy and gladness,
  and sorrow and sighing shall flee away.
                            Isaiah 51.11 RSV

FORGIVENESS

*Be kind to one another, tender-hearted,
forgiving one another as God in Christ
forgave you.*

Ephesians 4.32 RSV

WHO DO I NEED TO FORGIVE?
HOW CAN I?

Nothing in this world bears the impress of the Son of God so surely as forgiveness.
Alice Cary

Forgiveness sounds a fine principle, but I don't feel like forgiving. When someone's been hurt like I've been hurt, forgiveness is the last thing on the agenda. It really hurts, LORD. It's as if I've been devalued. It feels as though the bitterness grows, as though the resentment is getting in the way of my making progress.

I'd like to be rid of these feelings, to feel better. It's as though not being able to forgive hinders my own healing. I'd like to sort it; but they aren't sorry (well, they haven't said so to me), so why, LORD, should I have to make the first move?

MY CHILD, I hear the yearning of your heart; the pain in your soul echoes like nails being driven in. I hear your desire to be able to sort it despite your hurting. Let me turn your desire into a decision; to give my Spirit of reconciliation and peace, that you may have a way forward.

In particular, nursing resentments and lack of forgiveness to any who have wronged us can be powerful blocks to (our) healing.
Burrswood healing service

I can help you choose to forgive – let the desire become an intention of your heart.

LORD, can it really be enough to decide to forgive? Don't I have to do anything?

MY CHILD, in that decision you can tell me that, whether you feel like it or not, you choose to love, or to go on loving them, despite the fact you've been so hurt by them.

Real forgiveness used to be my right alone. Now I share it with my friends: when you don't feel like that sort of love, please ask me for the grace to choose to treat them as if you loved them.

But, LORD, we are so far apart.
It seems so long ago.
What can I do? What can I say?

MY CHILD, whatever else you may find to do or say, bring them to me. In your mind's eye, bring them before my cross: see my saving, healing, forgiving love rest upon them. Hold them there, for me to bring peace. Then, I promise you, you will find yourself receiving my forgiveness and healing in your turn, melting away any resentment or hardness of heart. I will enter your life again, in a new way, letting you use and enjoy my saving grace.

FORGIVENESS

Lord Jesus, you know how I feel about them, and what I've suffered at their hands.

I confess my feelings to you, especially anything which prevents the flow of your mercy and grace.

I offer to you my desire to be able to forgive.

I pray you, by your Holy Spirit, convert my desire to a decision; in your graciousness show me what I may say or do that will convey loving kindness from me, despite the hurt that I feel. Show me how to behave as if I have love for them.

Grant, then, that I may have the faith and courage to follow the way you show and, in offering forgiveness myself, be open to receive the forgiveness and healing love you have for me.

In the meantime, dear Lord, I picture your embrace of them, bringing with it the assurance of your love and forgiveness offered, without condition, through the cross.

Convey, I pray, something of my desire to be reconciled, whether it is recognised or not.

Thank you, Jesus.   I trust you.

Amen

PRAYER FOR FAMILY
AND FRIENDS

*The only way to
have a friend is
to be one.*
Ralph Waldo
Emerson

My family and my friends come to my
mind. How good they are!

I fear that I am becoming self-absorbed,
egocentric; it is often my own problems
which are on my mind. But these others
have problems, too.
Me, for one!
They need grace in time of need . . . my
need and their own.

I look at them when they come to see
me. They look me over; they assess what
to say.
They need to be themselves! I must tell
them so.

And they need me to take an interest in
them!
I always was struck by the patients who,
in the midst of their pain and sickness,
ask, 'How are you this morning, Doctor?'

Real friends warm you by their presence, trust you with their secrets, and remember you in their prayers.

Yes; I need them, but they need me too. They need my blessing, they need my love, my gratitude, my friendship, my warmth of affection, my assurance that they can go! – 'I'll be fine: you go. You've done me proud.'

How can I tell my family that I love them? My mind ranges through the possibilities. I could say it again. But it's familiar territory; would they even notice?
'Go and have a meal on me. If anyone deserved it, it's you.' Hmm. I wonder.
God grant me new ways of loving them! – new ways to replace the old ways, the ways I can't do any more, to keep the fire alive.

And my friends: how can I be a blessing? These special ones who have stuck by me, and in whose presence I am warmed. I cannot join them in the same way; I am not their equal any more. I shall write down all the ways I can bless them . . .

I can pray. Lord, bless them, Lord, be close to them. Give them your joy, your peace . . .

'Woman, behold your son!' Then he said to the disciple, 'Behold, your mother!'
John 19.26 RSV

I think of Jesus, on the cross, in his agony; he looks at his mother. May my love be like his, in my weakness and my pains.

PRAYERS FOR FAMILY AND FRIENDS

. . . we have not ceased to pray for you.
We ask God our Father that you may receive
from him full insight into his will, all
wisdom and spiritual understanding, so that
your manner of life may be worthy of the
Lord and entirely pleasing to him. We pray
that you may bear fruit in active goodness
of every kind, and grow in the knowledge
of God.

Colossians 1.9–10 REB

I thank my God
every time I think
of you; whenever I
pray for you all,
my prayers are
always joyful.
Philippians 1.3–4
REB

Loving God, our Father, you are worthy of all thanksgiving and praise. We thank you that we can come in prayer to you, and in obedience to Jesus ask all that is on our hearts for those we love and care for. We must express our gratefulness for so many blessings.

In gladness I picture Jesus in the Holy Family, an example blessed by your presence and love.

In gratitude I hear him teach us to pray for each other to you, Father of us all.

In delight I realise he means our prayer to be a sharing of our mutual concerns and cares, seeking for your Kingdom to come.

Loving God, our Father, giver of life and faith, may there be joy and confidence in our prayers, even though this is a time of difficulty and disease, when some of us are hurting badly. Lord, like the Psalmist we cry out at all times of day and night. It's strange how we are reminded of people. When we think of them, please make that thought a prayer for them to be helped.

In obedience to you I pray for my neighbours: the more I get to know them the more I want them to be touched by your spirit and your saving love.
I pray for the ones nearest to my heart; so aware of their deeper feelings, fears and hopes, I implore you again to meet them with your comfort and love just when and where they need it most. And when it is very difficult to be in contact, please convert the sighings of our souls into prayers with which you touch us in the spirit.

Now and in the longer term I pray for the youngsters I know. What will your world be like when they celebrate their eightieth birthdays? May it still be your year for them, Father of us all; may there always be someone to intercede for them.

Father, hear us; Father, graciously hear us.

Loving God, our Father, your will is to give health and salvation; as we pray to you for our friends, grateful for their sharing and support, we have to confess we have not always kept well in touch and have lost contact with some.

In your great mercy, Father of all, make up for the shortcomings in our relating to each other; may we share understanding and appreciation of one another.

In the depth of my heart, Father, I know there are some folk I need to forgive. It is a real struggle to forgive those whose treatment and actions I resent. Enable me, I pray, to choose to regard them with the love that only you can engender: release me thus from the bonds of hard-heartedness, to enjoy the fruits of reconciliation and forgiveness in my own life.

Father, hear us; Father, graciously hear us.

Loving God, our Father, gentle and merciful, hear our prayers for all whom we bring to you in Jesus' name; for the ones we picture readily before you, and those whom it is not easy to recall. In the fullness of time complete your healing work in them; let them be aware that your grace and love are sufficient, even in the darkest day.

In their needs, whether rejoicing by a crib, or aching by a cross, whether in sickness or sorrow, whether greeting new opportunities or facing creaky relationships – Father, be real to them with the signs of Jesus' salvation, for today and for ever.

In all of this, our Father God, I know there is nothing better I can do than hand them all over to you, for in your power and your good will I trust. When I picture them now, it will be with Jesus, taken up in the warmth and light of your love, freshness and liveliness. Thank you – thank you – thank you. Amen

FACING THE FUTURE
WITH HOPE

*May the God of hope fill you with all joy
and peace in believing, so that by the power
of the Holy Spirit you may abound in hope.*
Romans 15.13 RSV

*Behold the eye of
the Lord is upon
them that fear
him,
upon them that
have hope in his
mercy.
For our heart shall
rejoice in him,
because we have
trusted in his holy
name.*
Psalm 33.18, 21 AV

To say, 'Today is the first day of the rest of
my life,' does not mean that whatever has
gone before is irrelevant or has no influ-
ence or meaning. We step into the future
neither unformed nor uninformed by
our past. Our experience tells us that we
can never be sure about the future; but
perhaps that experience can give us hope
for what is to come. Part of that experience is our relationship with God.

*We rest in the
faith of yesterday
and wait for the
return of God.*
Russell Hicks

The last five verses of Psalm 33 are worth
reading right through, emphasising the
present moment of living hopefully,
knowing we are under God's ever watch-
ful and protective eye. Having trusted
him in the past we are confident of
rejoicing in him in the future. In Psalm
71 we find the life of praise and trust

issues into a continuing hope. Even Jeremiah, hardly one to be described as a natural optimist, prophesied in a wonderful canticle, 'There is hope for your future' (31.17).

If, however, too many of our recent yesterdays have been bad days, with precious few indications of God's likely return, keeping tattered faith intact can become a lonely ordeal. And if recent news has been bleaker than usual the future can look like that dark night which causes heart-wrenching trepidation. To speak of hope when the outlook is truly threatening can sound like denial: in these situations sharing the awe-full truth of our deeper feelings may be the only way to retain meaningful contact – with loved ones, with our own souls, even with the Almighty.

Dear friends in Corinth!
We have spoken frankly to you; we have opened our hearts wide.
2 Corinthians 6.11
GNB

If St Paul was as open and forthright to God in his personal prayers as he was to other Christians in his letters, he will have been very explicit indeed. To the Corinthians he wrote of many hardships, privations and threats of death; he illustrated his point by showing his own weakness as proof of God's power. He was very down to earth and practical, and his letters are as full of hope as they are of faith and love. In prison, on the brink of untimely execution, he could write:

My deep desire and hope is that I shall never fail in my duty, but that at all times, and especially just now . . . I shall bring honour to Christ, whether I live or die.
Philippians 1.20 GNB

Out of plain speaking comes a determined and pragmatic approach, both to friends and to the Lord. Such openness allows for a wrestling with the deep theological issues and an understanding of very particular needs. Living day by day when facing an uncertain or painful future, our need is for prayer for help and hope to be expressed in concrete terms.

As Henri Nouwen, the Dutch Catholic priest, put it:

This concreteness is even a sign of authenticity. For if you ask only for faith, hope, love, freedom, happiness, modesty, humility, etc. without making them concrete . . . you probably haven't really involved God in your real life. But if you pray in hope, all those concrete requests are merely ways of expressing your unlimited trust in him who fulfils all his promises, who holds out for you nothing but good, and who wants for himself nothing more than to share his goodness with you.

It is when God appears to abandon us that we must abandon ourselves most wholly to God.
Archbishop François Fénélon

The God whom we address in this way is the one who has made himself known in the full substance of human flesh and bone, in emotion and torment in the incarnation of Christ. On the cross, facing the bleakest of earthly futures in the fulfilment of his vocation Jesus cried out, 'My God, my God, why have you forsaken me?' Yet within minutes he was heard to pray, 'Father, into your hands I commend my spirit.'

FACING THE FUTURE
WITH HOPE

*I know what I have believed
and am persuaded that he is able to keep
what I have committed to him until that
day.*

2 Timothy 12.6 RAV

*My God, my God,
why have you
forsaken me?*
Mark 15.34 NIV

David was direct with you, O Lord.
> Paul prayed explicitly, my Saviour.
>> And I, too, need to be completely
open before you
>>> for my desire is to be known
by you, and to know you.

*Thus says the Lord
to Hezekiah; 'Set
your house in
order, for you shall
die and not live'.
Then he turned
his face to the
wall, and prayed
to the Lord . . .
and wept . . .
'I have heard your
prayers, I have
seen your tears . . .
And I will add to
your days fifteen
years . . .'*
2 Kings 20.1–6

Hear, then, my heart's cry which
> I pour out before you.
You know; yet I need to voice my fears
> my anxieties
>> my dread
>>> my sense of alone-ness
knowing you understand.

I have sought to be before you; to be and
> not to do.
And now, as I face the future, I cannot
> feel certain that
my being will continue as I know it.
> I might separate, my body into death,
> my soul unto you.
>> And I am afraid of the
separation.

Then the dust will return to the earth as it was, and the spirit will return to God who gave it.
Ecclesiastes 12.7
RAV

I know you might heal me, O Lord, you who gave Hezekiah fifteen more years before he had to face the separation.

Yet he did.
Like an egg, he separated. I am afraid.

My Lord, my God, do you love me?
  My hope is in your love!
Do you wrap your arms around me, your
  bleeding arms?
Does your heart yearn for me, your
  broken heart?

God so loved the world that he gave his only begotten Son, that whosoever believeth in him should not perish, but have everlasting life.
John 3.16 AV

Am I 'whosoever'? Lord, I run to you,
  I place my trust in you again! – and
  again! – and again!
For I know that if I can trust you even in
  my separation
I can trust you in all.
My heart is warmed.
    My hope is in you. O Lord my God!
      Hold me; do not let me go.
        You are my rest for ever.
In you will I dwell.

COURAGE

Be strong and of good courage;
be not frightened, neither be dismayed;
for the Lord your God is with you wherever
you go.

Joshua 1.9 RSV

. . . the sick
person is
normally not very
brave.
Dr Heije Faber

Fine words – if you are feeling fine. But when you face something threatening and unknown, to be courageous is easier said then done.

Even people who are usually strong and not easily daunted have their moments when courage is thin. Many of us seem to suffer more in the dark hours, when sleep feels far away.

As to moral
courage,
I have very rarely
met with two
o'clock in the
morning courage:
I mean
unprepared
courage.
Napoleon

If we cannot evade these moments from whom can we find encouragement?

The experience of Gethsemane shows God is with us; and is able to give a promise.

He did not say, 'You shall not be tempted;
you shall not be travailed;
you shall not be afflicted.'
But he said, 'You shall not be overcome.'
Julian of Norwich

God gives his angels charge over those who sleep. But he himself watches with those who wake.
Ugo Bassi

Thus we may address what needs to be overcome.

In daily life, or when times are tough, it is not so black and white. We are liable to be pulled one way and the other, forgetting the source of our help.

> *When we feel us too bold, remember our own feebleness.*
> *When we feel us too faint, remember Christ's strength.*
> Thomas More

Courage faces fear and thereby masters it. Cowardice represses fear and is mastered by it.
Martin Luther King

Matthew Fox said that facing the darkness, admitting the pain, allowing the pain to be pain, is never easy; that is why courage – big-heartedness – is the most essential virtue on the spiritual journey. Having a big heart allows us to meet our foe head-on yet without collision.

By perseverance the snail reached the Ark.
Charles Spurgeon

Yet there is more: it was Samuel Johnson who thought that great works are performed not by strength but by perseverance.

Nothing is as strong as gentleness. Nothing so gentle as real strength.
François de Sales

So God brings us to a safe place, where we can feel fortified and comforted. But his gifts of courage and comfort are for a purpose.

> *God does not comfort us to make us comfortable, but to make us comforters.*
> John Jowett

COURAGE

Father, hear the prayer we offer:
Not for ease that prayer shall be,
But for strength that we may ever
Live our lives courageously.

Maria Willis

Fatherly God, I praise you that when I feel unsafe in myself I may be sure of you: the one to whom I may come for security, comfort and strength.

Fatherly God, in you I find my hope and my resource; in you I can trust. When I do not know where to turn, you will seek me out as a shepherd finds the lamb that is lost.

Fatherly God, your perfect love overcomes in me the dread that lurks in the darkness, and the sickness that comes suddenly in the daytime.

Fatherly God, I thank you that from your heart of love you give us the courage we need in the face all that threatens us.

Be our strength in hours of weakness, In our wanderings be our guide; Through endeavour, failure, danger, Father, be thou at our side.
Maria Willis

this day draws on, Father, I trust in your might, in the grace of Jesus our risen Lord and in the comfort of your Holy Spirit. I pray you for myself, and others I know in much the same boat as I, and for my dear ones: may we know and enjoy your protection, your help and your deliverance from all that would come against us.

Strong in the everlasting name, And in my Father's care, I trust in him, I trust in him who hears and answers prayer.
Timothy Dudley-Smith

If it should be discomfort or pain may we meet it neither grumbling nor complaining; if it should be uncertainty or long delays may we meet it with hope and patience; if it should be sudden fear or loneliness may we meet it bravely and with faith.

Even if I go through the deepest darkness, I will not be afraid, Lord, for you are with me. Your shepherd's rod and staff protect me.
Psalm 23.4 GNB

Lighten our darkness, we beseech you, O Lord; and by your great mercy defend us from all perils and dangers of this night; for the love of your only Son, our Saviour, Jesus Christ. Amen

TIREDNESS AND WEAKNESS

My strength has drained away like water –
it has dried up like sunbaked clay.

Psalm 22.14–15 Living Bible

God comes in
where my
helplessness
begins.
Oswald Chambers

We all know feelings of tiredness. A bout of the flu leaves us weak at the knees and feeling worn out when we try to do even a limited amount: we wait for a while, and then our energy returns. Suddenly vitality comes back and we, if reflective and prayerful, thank God for it. Life has a cutting edge again, and we can be productive.

But serious illness, or even certain treatments, can precipitate a deeper tiredness, malaise, and weariness. Like a cloud it envelops and entraps, and makes our world a smaller place. It is the degree to which this profound malaise can affect us which is the surprise. Most patients with terminal illness and constant fatigue cite this as the symptom that distresses them most.

So how do we respond to this most distressing symptom? We pray, and God in his goodness may grant us help, in the form of healing, or of grace to bear our load. God is our strength; so the Psalmist cries out – 'O God, my strength, help me,' (Psalm 22.19) – and so we also cry to him, for he alone is able to help.

Our weaknesses make us appreciate God's strength.
Erwin Lutzer

'O God, my strength: let your strength flow over me, that I might become strong in you'.

Then we trust our times are in his hands, and he knows when our lives will end: we can only determine that the living he grants we live for him. And so in our weakness we can find a resolve: 'What I live, I will live for him'. Yet in the weakness of this simple resolve is great power, life and freedom.

There are seldom good reasons for suffering; but there can be good responses.
David Watson

The reality is that we have a deep and abiding need to live close to the Lord; in the rush and bustle of life the reality often passes us by. But now in our weakness, to whom shall we turn? What is God to us? And how might we draw close enough to drink of his strength and his life?

It must be partly by faith in his love for his child in need, and partly by doing those things which, left undone, keep us unaware of his love, and his presence. Like forgiving, and apologising, and repenting – all forbidding words which blossom to life as they are enacted. An elderly gentleman, realising his passing was approaching, wrote a letter which he sent to many, confessing that he had at times been cantankerous, and beseeching forgiveness in the spirit of love. That letter was pure joy to those who received it, and a source of blessing for the old man through the affection and forgiveness it generated. It is an example for us.

TIREDNESS AND WEAKNESS

My grace is sufficient for you . . .

2 Corinthians 12.9 RSV

Lord,
>I remember when life was vibrant
>And my being pulsated with
>strength;
>>I leaped from rock to rock
>>>and I was as strong as I
>>>was supple.

I remember;
>and now I am invaded by weakness.
>I stumble across my room;
>>I am as weak as I am stiff.

Lord, help me!
>Save me from myself.
>Save me from envy,
>>save me from bitterness,
>>>save me from being
>>>self-absorbed,
>>>>for it is too small a
>>>>place for my soul.

Forgive us our
trespasses, as we
forgive those who
trespass against
us.

Lord, show me the way.
 I would be forgiven: lead me in the
 ways of forgiveness, and
  lead me in the ways of humility,
  into all your ways.

Lord, show me your Kingdom
 For you make it mine – mine!
 Hallelujah! – it is my home!
  Into the greyness – Lord! – shine
  your wonderful light!
   Let it shine into my being, and
    let it shine through
    my eyes.
     Let all who come
     see it, and
      make me a sign-
      post to life indeed–
       life eternal.
Through Jesus Christ our Lord and
Saviour.

Amen

ACCEPTANCE

*God, give us grace to accept with serenity the
things that cannot be changed, courage to
change the things that should be changed,
and the wisdom to distinguish the one from
the other. Amen*

Reinhold Niebuhr

*Wishful thinking
plays a
considerable part
in the life of the
sick.*
Dr Heije Faber

Acceptance is not the same as fatalism. It
is possible to appear to accept a situation, while hiding from the truth of what
is going on; without wanting to know the
details, looking almost anywhere but at
reality. It can be denial to say, *Que sera
sera.* It carries with it the dangers of pre-
tence, unresolved anger and fear, separation from others without real sharing,
and can be just a cop-out. Rejection of
the facts can show itself in a number of
ways.

*Christianity is
about acceptance,
and if God accepts
me as I am
then I had better
do the same.*
Hugh Montefiore

Acceptance is much more than a sullen
resignation to the inevitable or a with-
drawal from engagement, living in a soli-
tary bubble of pseudo peace. It is a
challenge to allow the truth, face issues,
meet reality, gain knowledge, seek
resources to come to terms with affliction, negotiate a relationship with the situation. It sounds a tall order; there feels
to be a danger of being overwhelmed.

Where can one find the grace and perseverance for this on one's own?

Perhaps a genuine faith offers a way to accept reality. A Macmillan Nurse suggested that a patient treat her affliction as a gift. Taking up this possibility transformed her attitude to her illness, enabling her to receive, possess and use her sickness for good, sensing some meaning in what was happening. Such a view of the given in the situation allows a choice to live constructively despite the constraints, making reconciliation with others, seeking to live within the will of God, committed to him.

Acceptance says, 'True, this is my situation at the moment. I'll look unblinkingly at the reality of it. But I'll also open my hands to accept willingly whatever a loving Father sends.' Catherine Marshall

To be ready to accept willingly whatever God sends need not imply that we believe he has explicitly caused our sickness. But it does open us to receiving the fullness of his love and power to live through and overcome the dreadfulness in the afflictions we endure. Jesus chose and accepted the divine will as the only effective, righteous way out of the awfulness of Gethsemane; consequently our redemption was worked. Let us grasp his will, praying he may use us to strengthen, endorse and enhance his Kingdom. Then our acceptance may bring us deep peace.

ACCEPTANCE

Though our outer nature is wasting away, our inner nature is being renewed day by day.
2 Corinthians
4.16

Dear Lord,
    I would rather not face this.
They are all explaining it to me – in
words of one syllable, so that I can
understand.
    I *can* understand: but I am still not
    sure that I *want* to.
So for now, I am looking away.
    I don't want to accept.
        Yet I don't want to reject . . .

My Lord,
    once I accept, I shall have to change . . .
        my self-image
        my plans
            even perhaps my
            delusions of immortality.
Nothing will be the same again.

'Except me.'

You will be the same, Lord?
'And we shall walk together.'

You will not abandon me?
'Never, never, never.'

Lord, then grant me courage to reach out
to you; and accept.
  Let us be close: may I feel your
  presence.
Hold me and enfold me;
fill me with your Spirit;
  renew me and make me more
  like you
    day by day.

And, Lord, grant me courage to live
for you
  while I have breath in my body.
Let me love with your love,
  speak with your voice,
    do all you want me to do
as we face the future – together.

Lord, I accept.

PEACE OF MIND

Jesus spoke . . . and there was a great calm.

Luke 8.24

Seek peace and pursue it.
Psalm 34.14

Where is the calm for us?
When we are tossed about on the waves of uncertainty – where is the calm?
Peace of mind is so often like a butterfly. It flits into our field of view in all its beauty. It flits out again. We register its existence: but we are faced with the indigestible meal of our own problems.

Where can I go from your Spirit? Where can I flee from your presence?
Psalm 139.7

We do not follow peace. We do not pursue it.

Where then is our peace of mind? It is not in our problems. It is not even in the solution of our problems, ultimately. They are temporal. Even Lazarus, who was raised to life, had to die again after a while.

Rise up, my love, my fair one, and come away . . .
Song of Solomon 2.10

No, our peace is in resting in a special place, the place of God's love. Like a bird with a broken wing in the hands of its rescuer, its deliverer, its healer, we struggle. But perhaps we would do better to worship. To turn our eyes upon the King, the Saviour, the lover of our souls, and let our fretful worryings cease. Turn our eyes upon Jesus . . .

So if you have been raised with Christ, seek the things that are above, where Christ is, seated at the right hand of God. Set your mind on things that are above, not on things that are on earth, for you have died, and your life is hidden with Christ in God.
Colossians 3.1–3

Worry is natural. Worship is supernatural; it is an activity born of faith. Worry brings us down. Worship lifts us up.

We should worship more than we worry. So we lift up our eyes to the King. We seek those things which are above, where Christ is . . .

There is our peace. There is our calm.

PEACE OF MIND

*May God our Father and
the Lord Jesus Christ
give you grace and peace.*

St Paul, in these or very similar words,
in thirteen letters

*'Peace be with
you.'*

Dear Lord, I am so glad that it is from you that all thoughts of truth and peace come; so glad that for someone like Paul it was just perfectly natural to greet people with a prayer for grace and peace. I need to make a prayer for peace in my life; I could do with having you, Lord Jesus, come right now to speak into my turmoil.

*'My peace I give
to you, my peace I
leave with you.'*

Bless you, dear Lord, for that greeting – the one that calmed the fears of my forebears, the apostles. It is not just the worries and anxiety, Lord: it's the way I let them get to me, getting me agitated and upset, that I have to confess. I need your pardon and peace, so that I can feel cleansed and free to serve you with a quiet mind. Lord, have mercy: let me know deep down that your peace is there for me.

*'You will have
peace by being
united to me. The
world will make
you suffer.
But be brave!
I have defeated
the world.'*

Bless you, dear Lord, for your peace is so different from other people's gifts of peace: it goes deeper. My heart need not be troubled, even though I get very confused. I am so easily distracted by the ordinary aches and pains; itchings and irritations disturb me in the flesh. To set my mind on the Spirit is easier said than done, even though I recall that your Word promises life and peace this way. I pray you, Lord, remind me.

'Peace, be still.'

Bless you, dear Lord, that you come to me; speak to me, that through your Holy Spirit I may experience your living presence, and your most excellent gifts of love, joy and peace. Help me, Lord, to let go of the desires and distractions of the heart, and centre my gaze on you, hearing your word as you bring your moments of calm into the middle of the storms of my life.

*'Your faith has
healed you: go in
peace.'*

Bless you, dear Lord, for the effect of your peace, good news that quietens my soul. I realise it is deep down that I need to let your word bring that perfect peace which is your Shalom, your wholeness, your completeness of faith and healing grace. I put my self into your hands, Lord, for the assurance of your word of peace.

*'Your faith has
saved you: go in
peace.'*

Bless you, dear Lord: indeed your peace is beyond all understanding. You, Lord, are keeping me, heart and mind, safe in your love. Alleluia! Amen

NEARING THE END

*For God so loved the world that he gave his
only Son, that whoever believes in him shall
not perish, but have everlasting life.*

John 3.16 RAV

*Precious in the sight of the Lord is the death
of his saints.*

Psalm 116.15 AV

I am afraid. Shall I recover? Is this the
time for laying down this weak and
weary body?

I stand on the edge of human experience
and peer into the unknown.

All that is within me hopes for the everlasting arms of the God of Love: I ponder
and meditate on this great passage of
Scripture.

God so loved the world. God so loved me.

Whoever believes. I believe.

Shall not perish. I shall not perish, but have everlasting life.

Then why is it so hard?

I walk alone. None can come with me.
Yet you are with me, O Lord my God.
My loved ones are so distraught.
They can only wave me off on my journey.
Yet you can comfort them, O Lord.
My failures, my disappointments, flash
before me.
I wanted to do more for you, Lord.
Yet you know. You know my repentance and
my tears, and you forgive.
Forgive. Forgive.

You whom I have wronged: I long to make all things right. Forgive me, I ask.

Release me: I am so sorry.

You whom I have loved: do not fear. God is with me and will be with you.

I am ready, O Lord. In your time, in your mercy, in your peace,

Let me to your bosom fly.

NEARING THE END

The last enemy to be defeated will be death.

1 Corinthians 15.26 GNB

*At all times we carry in our mortal bodies
the death of Jesus, so that his life also may
be seen in our bodies.*

2 Corinthians 4.10 GNB

Heavenly Father, as I near the end of my earthly time, I need your grace and support to watch and wait with faith and inner peace. Stay by me, and those who love or care for me, I pray.

We need your help and strength to let each other go, after all we've shared and all we've meant to each other. But let us not feel alone from each other, I pray.

We need your courage to let go of the last lingering hopes of a miracle. Comfort us in this moment, I pray.

Heavenly Father, though it seems we've said all we can, I confess there still feels like unfinished business to be done. When I can no longer 'get through' I still want to speak out, and yet I doubt I 'get through'. Then, Lord, I pray, by your Holy Spirit convey to the depths of the other's spirit all that I want to convey: my farewells, my goodbyes and my love.

To you, dear Lord, I want to say: let me 'fare well' in your eternal light. Let me come gently and fare well with you. Lord, be so close that I know the true reality of your presence, to take away all fears, and just let you take over, holding me in calmness and light.

Heavenly Father, I need you to be with those who love me too, that they may fare well, for they are handling a mix of strong feelings; pray grant them clarity and calm in the confusion.

In the awesome moment of my departure, pray grant them your steadiness when the shock comes. Lord, may they cope sensibly when there are things to be done.

Although I trust your grace, it seems as though the insecurities remain. I struggle to accept it all. As Jesus gave Mary and John to comfort each other by the cross, grant someone upon whose shoulder they and I may weep.

Heavenly Father, I confess there are moments when I wish it were all over: can it be wrong to pray you to fulfil your will? Lord, let release come from this last struggle, so that life may be complete.

Now, Lord, I can do no more: let this, your beloved servant, depart in peace. Pray take me into the hands of your mercy. I can do no more.

Fatherly God, I commend myself:
    into your merciful hands,
    into the radiance of your light,
    into the totality of your love,
    into the holiness of your presence,
    into the glory of your eternity.

Rest eternal grant to me, O Lord.
Let light perpetual shine upon me.

Amen. Amen. Amen.

RESTING IN CHRIST

Peace I leave with you; my peace
I give to you;
not as the world gives do I give to you.
Let not your hearts be troubled, neither let
them be afraid.

Jesus (John 14.27 RSV)

For as soon as we stop, the anguish creeps in and the guilt resurfaces.
Jean Vanier

'Be not afraid.' The most repeated command in the Bible is, 'Fear not.' How frequently in times of stress or sickness, whether in ourselves or loved ones, do apprehensions and anxieties drive our agitations into over-activity – of some sort, of any sort. To be not doing anything, not doing enough, is to feel condemned. This age is a frantic age, fraught with effort and business. Much of our response to disease is expressed in the language of striving, struggle, and battle. Too often the conflict within becomes reflected in conflict with others. And we dare not stop the feverish activity.

But at some stage we need to find the courage to stop;
to rest, to look at life . . .
try new ways to find peace of heart and a little tranquillity . . .
Jean Vanier

It feels as though the only alternative to this giddy-go-round is to give up, or give in, slipping into the lethargy of systems depressed. When wise voices say, 'Let go', it sounds like a counsel of defeat, or despair. Casting oneself adrift into what look like swirling waters never seems common sense.

Turn your eyes upon Jesus, Look full in His wonderful face; And the things of earth will grow strangely dim In the light of His glory and grace.
Helen H. Lemmel

. . . you will experience God's peace, which is far more wonderful than the human mind can understand. His peace will keep your hearts quiet and at rest as you trust in Christ Jesus.
Philippians 4.7
Living Bible

He will keep in perfect peace all those who trust in him, whose thoughts turn often to the Lord!
Isaiah 26.3 Living Bible

New ways; or old ways renewed. Recall how Christ approached disciples in a small boat on a stormy sea; soon they heard his words, 'Peace, be still.' His word was spoken with the same authority as when he met their fears on Easter Day with the greeting, 'Peace be with you.' When they heard those words they must have been face to face with Christ, perhaps looking into his eyes. Is this the clue to what sounds an impossible option in the face of pain and terror?

In faith we may have been conscious of Christ at our side; we may have laboured with Christ as our support. It is different to choose to look directly to him, face to face with Jesus, to be detached from other considerations, to let the reality of his light and his words sink into us as we offer our whole attention, open to the fullness of his presence and love. Our view can be transfigured and our lives transformed.

The way of adoration, leading into contemplation, is a different way: it is neither the desperate struggle nor the despairing resignation. It is facing a new way, into the deeper reality of Christ's looking at us with compassion and with his all-embracing yet liberating love setting us free to rest in his Shalom. Rest in him, rest on him. Then we hear in our heart his words of peace and calm assurance, real beyond our imagining.

RESTING IN CHRIST

I need rest: I need it as I need breath, for
without it I feel breathless.
Without it, I run, I run – whether in body
or mind matters not: I run.
And I do not find you.

The real problem of the Christian life . . .
comes the very moment you wake up each
morning. All your wishes and hopes for the
day rush at you like wild animals. And the
first job each morning consists of simply
shoving them all back; in listening to that
other voice, taking that other point of view,
letting that other larger, stronger, quieter life
come flowing in. And so on, all day.
          C. S. Lewis, from *Mere Christianity*

My Lord, I fear that wild animals got me
today – though not all of them, for sometimes I remembered; I stopped, and in your
presence I did find a little tranquillity.
But Lord Jesus, you who were storm-
tossed and afflicted, I ask you: teach me
to find the still point in my soul.

O my soul, rest in Christ's will, knowing
that like a bottle in an ocean you are safe
and kept and will be washed up in the
right place, in the end.

Yet I am not a bottle. I need to see into
    your eyes, O Lord,
to see in them depth, the depths of love;
    and compassion. For me.
    I want to get lost in the depths;
    I want to run into your arms,
            to know your presence and your
            love. I'm coming!
                I want to be lost in our love,
                and I want you to receive
                mine,
                    small though it is,
                        that we might know
                        that communion
                        of love.
                        'Mary!' 'Master!'
Here is my rest.
    Here is my rest for ever, in this holy
    love.
        Let the storm rage: it is outside,
        and the doors and windows are
        shut.

THANKFULNESS

Give thanks to the Lord, call on his name;
make known among the nations
what he has done.
Sing to him, sing praise to him;
tell of his wonderful acts.

Psalm 105.1,2 NIV

There is a graciousness about thankfulness. We see it even in children. Those grateful for a gift, for a blessing, we long to bless: those reticent and surly, and slow in expressing thanks, we are tempted to withdraw our blessing from. There is a lesson here for us, and an encouragement to thankfulness as a way of life.

Yet can we be thankful for blessing even in the midst of suffering? It is a further step, an evidence of God's grace at work. We see so little – as through a glass darkly, as St Paul puts it: we cannot easily see God's purposes in our suffering. Elsewhere St Paul chides the Corinthians – 'You are looking only on the surface of things' (1 Corinthians 10.7 NIV). Suffering comes to us all, 'as the sparks fly upwards': happy are we if we can be thankful in spite of our troubles. We shall be an encouragement to many, as those thankful yet suffering souls we know are to us.

Heavenly Father,
grant me the
wisdom
to see the good
in everyone and
everything.
You know my
needs: I do not
need to ask.
I appreciate your
gifts. Amen
James Haylock
Eyre

The more I lose
my little skills,
The more I see
God's plan,
I see what really
counts with Him:
The essence of a
man.
James Haylock
Eyre

But thankfulness can reach extraordinary heights when it is unhinged from any obvious cause; when it says thank you in circumstances which defy natural gratitude. It then changes from a natural sentiment to a spiritual crown, an evidence of victory at the deepest level. It is born of faith. It says, 'I choose a different way; I choose to accept that God knows what he is doing and will work all things for my good – even though I do not now see it.' There is a majesty in it which humbles and moves us whenever we see it. It opens prison doors. It is the settling of eternal questions – the 'why?', the 'how long?' – and it extinguishes bitterness. It is a height indeed.

And I ask myself, as I must: where am I, with regard to thankfulness?

God is the great encourager; he hears our longings, and helps us get to where we want to be. Thank you, Lord.

THANKFULNESS

This is the day that you have made, O Lord;
we will rejoice and be glad in it.
You are our God and we will thank you;
you are our God and we will exalt you.
Psalm 118.24, 28 CW

We give thanks to you, O Lord, for you are gracious; your mercy endures for ever.

Lord God of all the earth and of all the heavens, may our thanksgivings rise to you as the smoke of the heavenly incense rises before your majesty with the prayers of the saints in heaven. You are worthy, in Jesus slain for our healing, to receive thanksgiving and honour and glory and praise! Receive, we pray, our offering of thanksgiving and worship, blessing and love.

We give thanks to you, O Lord, for you are gracious; your mercy endures for ever.

Lord God, from deeply grateful hearts:
where relief is known and fears are calmed;
when pains are gone and threats are lifted;
when healing is real and all feels well
with me, with us, within your world
then our thankfulness overflows.

We give thanks to you, O Lord, for you are gracious; your mercy endures for ever.

Lord God, from sorely tried minds:
through dark nights and chronic waitings;
when the disease is dire and prognosis poor;

when the spirit is low and prayers ring
unheard
in me, in us, in your world,
then we choose to make the sacri-
fice of thanksgiving
and offer our will to you,
O most high.

We give thanks to
you, O Lord, for
you are gracious;
your mercy
endures for ever.

Lord God, welling up in souls lifted to
the heights:
by your graciousness and your love;
by your encouragement and your help;
by your assurance and the reality of your
presence
given me, given us, given into your
world
then in joy and praise and
gratitude we hallow your name.

Our hearts enter
your gates with
thanksgiving, and
your courts with
praise.
We give thanks to
you and bless your
name. Amen

Great is our thankfulness, O God our
Father, for creation, protection and mercy;
real is our thankfulness, Jesus our
Saviour, in times of suffering and
healing;
deep is our thankfulness, divine Spirit,
for lively gifts and all inspiration;
full is our thankfulness, O Holy Trinity,
for promised wholeness and holiness.

INFORMATION ABOUT BURRSWOOD

The Burrswood Christian Centre for Healthcare and Ministry was founded some 50 years ago by the late Dorothy Kerin in fulfilment of a commission from God, 'to heal the sick, comfort the sorrowing and give faith to the faithless'. The community is dedicated to bringing together Christ's healing ministry and orthodox medical care. It is recognized as a centre of excellence and experience in this field.

At the heart of Burrswood is the Church where public healing services are offered. It is integrated with a 35-bed registered hospital, 16-bed guesthouse, hydrotherapy pool, bookshop and tearoom set in a 225-acre country estate on the edge of Ashdown Forest. Many who come for a short hospital stay are enabled to do so irrespective of their means.

People find God's healing power at work through skilled nursing, medical expertise, prayer ministry and counselling. The aim is to keep the love of Christ at the heart of true whole-person care and to be a sign of the kingdom of God in a hurting world. Stillness and beauty provide space for the Holy Spirit's transforming work in every area of life.

Burrswood
Groombridge
Tunbridge Wells
Kent, TN3 9PY

General enquiries: tel. 01892 863637
Enquiries about staying as a guest or admission as a patient:
tel. 01892 863818

www.burrswood.org.uk